CW00684345

# Crime and Punishment Through Time

## A STUDY IN DEVELOPMENT IN CRIME, PUNISHMENT AND PROTEST FOR SHP AND OTHER GCSE SYLLABUSES

Christopher Culpin

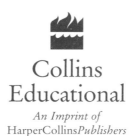

Collins
Educational
*An Imprint of*
HarperCollins*Publishers*

# CONTENTS

Crime, punishment and protest are controversial issues today. What kinds of crimes are increasing? Why are they increasing? What should we be doing about it? Should our punishments be tougher? Or easier?

Should we be building new prisons, like Woodhill in the picture below? What should we do with people, like the road protesters in the picture below, who break the law as a form of protest?

One of the reasons for studying History is that we can sometimes learn from the past. No two historical events are ever the same, but we can see how things might work out in the present by seeing what happened in the past.

In the first part of this book, called **The Story**, you will see what crime was like in the past, what punishments there were and how people protested. There are 'key questions' (marked ◆), to set up your investigation into each period, and other questions (marked ❖), to get you thinking. There are lots of historical sources because that is how historians find out about the past. Crime, punishment and protest are affected by what is happening in the rest of history, so each of the five chapters in **The Story** starts with some outline points to set the scene.

Historians are not just interested in *what* happened, they want to know *why*. In the second part of this book, called **Issues and Enquiries**, you will find examples of seven key factors which have affected crime, punishment and protest through time. You will also find examples of two different types of change.

You may be using this book to prepare for your GCSE examination. Depending on which syllabus you are following, you will select different sections of the book for study. You will find the timelines at the start of each chapter in **The Story** helpful when it comes to revision. You will also find sections called **Examining the Evidence** to give you some practice at Paper 2.

I hope you enjoy reading this book. This is a controversial topic and you will probably find it quite easy to tell what my opinions are on some topics. You do not have to agree with me, but I hope that your discussions will have more historical awareness as a result of reading it.

Christopher Culpin

# INTRODUCTION

This is a true story. In the spring of 1884, three men, Dudley, Stephens and Brooks, and a boy, Parker, set sail on their yacht, the *Mignonette*. Several days out at sea, there was a terrible storm. The *Mignonette* was wrecked and the four people hurriedly took to the lifeboat. They had no food or water. After 18 days adrift, all they had had to eat or drink was one turtle.

Dudley and Stephens then suggested to Brooks that one of the four should be killed (1) to provide food for the others. Brooks was horrified (2) and refused to take part when, on Day 20, Dudley and Stephens killed the boy, Parker. Over the next four days, all three men ate Parker's body and drank his blood. Then they were rescued.

On their return to England, Dudley and Stephens were put on trial for murder. They were found guilty (3) and sentenced to be hanged. The Queen pardoned them (4) and they served six months in prison instead.

**1** In dire situations like this there is really no law but the survival of the strongest. There have been times in History, as you will see in this book, particularly in the early part, when law has broken down. When that happens, it is the strongest, those who use force, who get their own way.

**2** Even in utmost necessity Brooks refused to be involved in killing Parker. He still had a sense of justice, of right and wrong (although he was prepared to eat Parker once the others had killed him). Throughout history, people have tried to have a code of laws based on this sense of what is right and wrong.

**3** The government insists on the law being enforced on its citizens, no matter what the situation. Dudley and Stephens argued in court that they had to kill to survive. The judge, Lord Coleridge, said that this was not an acceptable defence. Parker had done no wrong: who had the right to kill him? In this way governments have passed and enforced laws to a higher standard than just the survival of the strong.

**4** The monarch has the right to show mercy if the law seems unfair in certain specific cases.

*KEY QUESTIONS*
◆ *Who commits crimes?*
◆ *Why?*
◆ *How should they be punished?*

Read through the four cases on pages 5 and 6.
Use the lists on page 7 to reach your own decisions
about them.

## CASE 1

Vicky stole a child's coat from a shop. She is 18 years old and lives in a one-room bedsit with her two-year-old son, Joe.

The coat is valued at £15. Vicky had £1.90 on her at the time she committed the crime and says this is all the money she has. She normally manages on the money she receives, with some help from her mother, but says she could not afford to buy a coat for Joe. Vicky was a poor attender at school, and was involved in some minor vandalism at a sports club three years ago. She has never stolen anything before.

## CASE 2

Anthony is charged with assaulting Barry in a pub. They are both 22 years old. They had been friends as teenagers and had been in trouble with the police at that time for shoplifting. Since then they have drifted apart. Barry has not come to the notice of the police for any reason. Anthony is suspected of involvement in car thefts, but the police have not been able to prove anything.

On the night in question, both went to the pub separately, with different groups of friends. Anthony had a lot to drink and began making remarks about one of Barry's friends. Barry jokingly asked him to stop. Anthony became angry and suddenly attacked Barry with a broken glass. Barry's injuries needed 24 stitches.

## CASE 3

Michael is a company director, aged 48. He is married, with two children aged 15 and 11. He has a large house in the suburbs and he and his wife both have new cars. His children attend a private school. Up to three years ago his business was doing well and he had an expensive lifestyle, including membership of exclusive golf clubs. He was also known as a generous supporter of charitable causes.

Then his business began to go wrong. He made a number of bad deals and was cheated by one of his customers. He wanted to keep his children at their schools and to maintain the lifestyle he and his wife enjoyed, so he began to pay money due to the company into a separate bank account in his own name. He used his knowledge and experience of how the company worked to write false documents to cover up what he was doing. He did this for three years, taking larger and larger sums each time. In total he embezzled £550,000 over three years. In the end the tax inspector discovered what was happening and told the police.

## CASE 4

Jenny broke into an aircraft factory with a hammer and committed £10,000 worth of damage to the controls of a fighter aeroplane which was being built there and was nearly finished. She then rang the security alarm in order to get arrested. She says the plane was about to be sold to another country run by a dictator. He would use it to kill people protesting against his government. She admits the crime of damaging the plane, but says she was obeying a 'higher law' which justified it. In court she presented evidence that similar planes had been used by the dictator against unarmed civilians before.

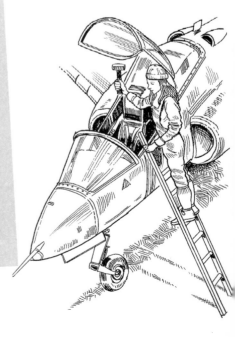

FOR EACH OF CASES 1 TO 4, USE THE LISTS
BELOW AND NOTE DOWN:
(A) What type of crime it is,
(B) What the motive was,
(C) What punishment you would recommend, and
(D) Why you recommend this punishment.

## (A) Types of crime

(i) **Crimes against the person**. For example, murder, rape, assault, armed robbery.
(ii) **Crimes against property**. For example, theft, robbery, burglary, poaching, smuggling, embezzlement, vandalism.
(iii) **Crimes of protest** against authority. For example, heresy, treason, strikes, sit-down protests.

NOTES:
1. Throughout history, there have always been five or ten times more crimes against property than crimes against the person. Crimes of protest are a very small proportion of all crimes committed.
2. Theft = taking someone else's property;
Robbery = using or threatening to use violence in order to commit a theft;
Burglary = entering a building in order to commit a crime, which may be theft, but also includes rape, damage to property or person.

## (B) Motives for crime

(i) **Need**. The person is too poor to buy what they want.
(ii) **Gain**. The person intends to sell the item stolen.
(iii) **Impulse**. The person acts on the spur of the moment, with no previous plan.
(iv) **Influences**. The person is under the influence of drugs or alcohol, or bad friends, or steals to get money to buy drugs or alcohol.
(v) **Belief**. The person believes the law is wrong.

## (C) Punishments

Here is a selection of punishments used at various times in history which you will find out about in this book:
(i) One year in prison
(ii) Cut off the criminal's hand
(iii) Prison with hard labour
(iv) Stand in the pillory (see page 37 for a picture of this)
(v) Pay money to the victim of the crime
(vi) 35 years in prison
(vii) Execution
(viii) Community service (see page 97 for what this means)
(ix) Go free
(x) Sent out of the country
(xi) Your own alternative punishment idea.

## (D) Purpose of punishment

(i) **Deterrence**. It will stop others doing the same thing.
(ii) **Removal**. It protects the public by removing the criminal.
(iii) **Punishment**. The criminal has a hard time, loses personal freedom, etc.
(iv) **Compensation**. The victim or society is paid back for the trouble they suffered from the criminal.
(v) **Reform**. The criminal changes his or her ways and will not commit any more crimes.
(vi) **Public shame**. The punishment is carried out in public so as to shame the offender.

# THE STORY 1
# THE ANCIENT WORLD

| | |
|---|---|
| **3000** | 3100 First Pharaohs unite Egypt |
| | 3000 First cities in Mesopotamia |
| | 2750 Civilisations in Indus Valley, India |
| **2500** | |
| **2000** | 2000 Civilisation in Crete |
| | 1700 Hammurabi founds Babylonian Empire and makes laws |
| | 1600 City civilisation in China |
| **1500** | |
| | 1200 Hebrews leave Egypt: Moses receives Ten Commandments |
| **1000** | |
| | 750 Greek city states flourish |
| **500** | 451 Twelve Tables of the Laws of Rome |
| | 290 Rome conquers all Italy |
| | 89 All Italians made Roman citizens |
| **0** | 43 AD Romans invade Britain |
| | 212 All inhabitants of Roman Empire made Roman citizens |
| | 330 Capital of Roman Empire moved to Constantinople |
| | 470 Rome sacked by Visigoths |
| **500** | 528 Justinian's Code of Roman Law |

## Early human beings

For hundreds of thousands of years humans lived in small groups. They moved around, hunting animals and gathering fruit, nuts, grains and leaves as they needed them. By about 8000 BC, humans were living in every continent except Antarctica.

## Farmers

From about 8000 BC humans began deliberately to plant and harvest cereal crops. They also domesticated animals. A better food supply could support more people, who lived settled lives in village communities. This happened first in Mesopotamia and in Central America, but then also in Egypt, West Africa, India and China.

## Cities and empires

Although the first city, Jericho, was established before 8000 BC, it was really after about 4000 BC that large towns and cities grew up in several areas. At the same time there was:

– **Trade**. In food and hand-made items, often over long distances, by land and by sea.

– **Rulers**. Empires, covering large areas, grew up under powerful rulers.

– **Writing**. More complicated ways of life, trade and government needed written records and communications.

## Rome

The greatest ancient empire in the Western World was the Roman Empire. Rome was founded in 756 BC and gradually expanded. At its greatest extent, in the 1st and 2nd centuries AD, Rome's empire stretched from Scotland to present-day Iraq. The Roman Empire in Western Europe collapsed in the 5th century AD.

# LAW IN THE ANCIENT WORLD

*KEY QUESTIONS*
◆ *What were the first laws?*
◆ *When were the first written laws?*

When humans lived in small groups, as wandering hunters or even as small farmers, they did not need many laws. Everyone knew how you were supposed to behave and disputes were few. Any disputes were settled, either by force, with the strongest people getting their own way, or by agreement, with the older and wiser members of the group making a judgement according to their customs.

The first sets of laws were needed when more people began to live in the first cities. This happened earliest in the great river valleys: in Egypt, Mesopotamia, in India and in China. With more people living close together, not everyone knew each other so well; land was valuable, so clear boundaries had to be drawn, and decisions made about who owned what.

Crimes were committed. Some people took to solving their disputes themselves, often violently, driven by revenge. Feuds grew up between families and tribes, sometimes lasting for years. Many people were killed. Chaos and fear threatened the new civilisations. The powerful rulers of these areas, the Pharaohs of Egypt, or the kings of Assyria or Babylon, had to keep the peace. They drew up laws, or collected the customs people were used to. Here are some important features of these laws:

● Rulers tried to ensure that they were widely known. The oldest surviving written set of laws can be seen in Source 1. Columns like this were set up all over Babylon. Alternatively, time was set aside to read the laws out loud to all the people (see Source 6).

● Rulers used their power to enforce the law and punish wrong-doers. Settling disputes was an important part of their task as ruler. Source 2 explains what Hammurabi saw as the purpose of his laws.

● Punishments may appear harsh to our eyes (see Source 3A), but at least the punishment is known, limited and ended there: it is not the start of an endless cycle of violent feuding. Nor is the idea of different punishments for rich and poor acceptable to us (Source 3B), but it recognised the realities of who held power. We shall see this feature again in this book.

**SOURCE 1**

Column showing the Laws of Hammurabi. It is 2.4m high and was put up in about 1700 BC. Hammurabi, ruler of Babylon, is standing on the left, receiving the laws from the Sun God, seated right, who holds a measuring rod and line, the symbols of order and fairness. There are 282 laws on the column, in 3,600 lines of writing.

● The laws are shown as coming, not from the minds of humans, but from God, or the gods. This gave them a weight and a timelessness and made them more likely to be obeyed.

## SOURCE 2

*An inscription on the column says that it was put up:*

To cause justice to prevail in the land, to destroy the wicked and the evil, that the strong might not oppress the weak.

## SOURCE 3

*Two of the laws of Hammurabi:*

A 'If a man has caused the loss of a man's eye, his own eye shall be lost. If he has broken a man's limb, one shall break his limb.'

B 'If he has caused a poor man to lose an eye, he shall pay one "mina" of silver.'

## SOURCE 4

And thine eye shall not pity, but life shall go for life, eye for eye, tooth for tooth, hand for hand, foot for foot.

*From the Bible, in the book of Deuteronomy, Chapter 19, verse 21.*

## SOURCE 5

1. You shall have no other gods before me.

2. You shall not make any graven image, nor any likeness of anything . . . you shall not bow down before them, nor serve them.

3. You shall not take the name of the Lord God in vain.

4. Remember the Sabbath day and keep it holy. Six days you shall work, but the seventh is the day of the lord God; in it you shall do no work.

5. Honour your father and your mother.

6. You shall not kill.

7. You shall not commit adultery.

8. You shall not steal.

9. You shall not bear false witness against your neighbour.

10. You shall not covet . . . anything that is your neighbour's.

*The Ten Commandments, from the Bible, the book of Exodus, Chapter 20 [adapted]. These were received from God by Moses, the Hebrews' leader, on Mount Sinai, in about 1300 BC.*

## The Hebrews

One of the most remarkable collections of early laws can be found in the Bible. The first six books of the Old Testament are the 'Torah', or law, of the Hebrews. These consist not just of the Ten Commandments (Source 5), but of some 613 laws. They were all God's wishes for the Hebrew people and took the prophet Ezra from early morning to midday to read (Source 6). They cover not just the kinds of things dealt with by our legal system but also many aspects of behaviour such as diet, dress and hospitality.

## SOURCE 6

And he [the prophet Ezra] read in the street that was before the watergate, from the morning until midday.

So he read in the book of the law of God, distinctly and gave the sense and caused them to understand the reading.

*From the Bible, in the book of Nehemiah, Chapter 8, verses 3 and 8.*

❖ *Look at Sources 4, 5 and 6. In what ways do the laws of the Hebrews follow the four features listed on page 10?*

❖ *Which of the Ten Commandments would we regard as laws, which as religious rules, and which as dealing with how people should treat each other?*

❖ *Why was writing the laws, or reading them out to the people (see Source 6), so important?*

# THE ROMANS AND THE LAW

**KEY QUESTION**

◆ *Was Roman Law fair?*

At the height of the Roman Empire, the city of Rome had about 1 million people, and no police. The Romans ruled an empire stretching from northern England to the Middle East, using the same laws. After the fall of the Roman Empire, Roman Law was taken on and used in Church courts, which played an important part in law and order in the Middle Ages (see Chapter 2). To this day, several countries, such as France, Scotland and South Africa, have a legal system based on Roman Law. Whatever else we can say about Roman Law, it seems to have been successful.

## The principles of Roman Law

One of the reasons for the success of Roman Law was that it was built on certain key principles:

**1.** Everyone is under the law. No one, not even an emperor or a slave, can claim to be above, below, or outside the law and so able to do what they like.

**2.** The law should be publicly known. The first Roman Law code was the Twelve Tables. These were inscribed on bronze sheets very early in the history of Rome, in 451 BC, and publicly displayed in the market-place. They were written because the ordinary Romans, the *plebs*, were annoyed that only upper-class Romans, who acted as judges, knew what the laws were.

The Twelve Tables covered all the basic legal issues as well as matters of planning and behaviour, such as how wide the roads in the city of Rome should be (4.8m) and whether senators ought to fart in public (they shouldn't). Many of the laws changed through Roman history, but Romans revered the Twelve Tables as their first public laws and they were used to teach children to read.

From 304 BC all legal decisions had to be published, so that people could see how the law was developing.

**3.** New laws should be rationally worked out from existing laws. As we saw on page 10, in most ancient civilisations law was based on religion – it was said to come from God (or the gods). Roman Law was not based on religion, but on logic and human reason.

**4.** The law should be seen to be carried out. Roman law-courts were open to the public and attracted many spectators.

**5.** People had the right to fair treatment from the law and, in serious matters, to be judged by their equals. Magistrates were supposed to treat everyone fairly (Source 1). No one could be sentenced to death without the right of appeal to the assembly of all citizens. You could also appeal to the emperor (Source 2). Most emperors took their legal duties very seriously.

### SOURCE 1

It is the duty of a magistrate to understand that he represents all citizens, and that he must therefore uphold the dignity and honour of the state, defend its laws, render justice and remember that all these powers have been entrusted to him as a sacred trust.

*Like many Roman politicians, Cicero made his early career in the law-courts. He also wrote about the law. Here he describes the duties of magistrates.*

### SOURCE 2

He once remained in court until nightfall and, if he was unwell, would have his bed carried to the court. Sometimes he even judged cases from his sickbed. As a judge he was careful, and lenient.

*The Emperor Augustus acting as a judge.*

### SOURCE 3

The basilica at Pompeii.

A 6th-century picture of a provincial governor sitting as a judge. In this case the Governor is Pontius Pilate, judging Jesus, although they are wearing clothes from the 6th century, rather than from Jesus' time.

## The courts

All the important officials who ran Rome, including running the law courts, were called **magistrates**. They were all elected. At first only members of the highest class, the senators, could stand for election, but this widened over time. The magistrate responsible for the laws was called the **praetor**.

Law-courts sat most days, except when important Games were on, from February onwards. No new cases started after October each year because they might go on beyond the period of office of one magistrate and into that of the new one, elected in January.

In cases between two people, for example property disputes or claims of damage to person or property, the praetor would first decide what the issues were in the case. He would then appoint a judge. The judge did not have to be a trained person, so would be helped by lawyers and by a jury of 50 to 80 people. The jury was also drawn from the higher classes, who saw it as one of their civic duties to serve the law-courts in this way.

In criminal cases another magistrate, called a **quaestor**, would hold an enquiry to see if there was a case to answer, and if so, what it was. (This is not the way English courts work, but is still used today in most of the countries that have a legal system based on Roman Law.)

## Law in the provinces

The law was administered by the governor of each province, who had already learnt something about it by serving as a praetor in Rome. He travelled around his province hearing cases (Source 4). Usually law-courts were held in the town's basilica (Source 3), where the governor would be surrounded by statues and symbols of Roman gods and emperors.

One of the reasons for the success of the Roman Empire was that it imposed the same system of laws all over the empire. Tricky questions of inheritance, marriage, business contracts, or injury could therefore all be settled by a known, respected and common set of laws.

Roman citizens were judged by Roman Law, and had the right of appeal to Rome. Non-Romans were judged by local laws, with legal experts trying always to reconcile local customs with the principles of Roman Law. In this way, these experts developed a kind of universal law, law which would apply to anyone. Their writings on the subject have become the basis of much later law-making, especially international law.

❖ *Look again at the five principles of Roman justice. What is the opposite of each? Why is each of them important for a just legal system?*
❖ *Do all the five principles apply to justice in Britain today? In what ways?*
❖ *Was the Roman legal system democratic?*

KEY QUESTION
◆ *Was Roman justice as good as the Romans liked to think?*

The Romans liked to boast of their achievements and many later writers have taken their claims at face value. Let us look at Roman law in a bit more detail and see how fair it really was.

## 1. Equal in law?

People living in Rome and the Roman Empire were not equal in law. In fact, a great deal of Roman law, from the Twelve Tables onwards, was designed to define and preserve these differences.

**(a) Romans and non-Romans**. As we have seen on page 13, Roman Law only applied to Roman citizens. In fact, the Romans were not racist about this. Black people and white, Italians and non-Italians, could all become citizens. Legally, it was one of the less important distinctions. Indeed, in 90 BC all Italians were made Roman citizens and in AD 212 virtually everyone in the Empire became Roman citizens.

**(b) Men and women**. A Roman woman had few rights at law, and could not appear in court, vote or become a magistrate. She could not own her own property and her inheritance rights were weak. In early Roman times her husband had the right of life or death over her. This situation improved slightly later, with women over 25 allowed to own property and the rights of widows and divorcees protected.

**(c) Slaves.** Ancient Rome was a slave-owning society. At least a quarter of the population of ancient Rome were slaves. Slaves had almost no legal rights: they could be bought and sold, killed, flogged; they could not own anything, marry or pass anything to their children. Again, the situation improved in the later Empire. Slaves gained some protection from their masters, the right to follow their own religion, and not to be thrown out when they became old or sick. Legal experts had difficulty with the idea of slavery and decided that it was not a natural state: people were naturally free – an important principle.

**(d) Classes** (or orders, as the Romans called them). The upper orders were usually richer, but money was not the real basis of the system. You were born into a particular order, with all the rights and duties of that order, and could not change. People in different orders wore togas with different colours, so that you could tell at a glance where someone was in the system. These divisions lasted as long as the Roman Empire and were enforced by the law.

● At the top were Senators. As we have seen, this order held almost all public offices (magistrates).

● Next came the *equites* or knights. They gained the right to become magistrates in the 2nd century BC. Some might be richer than senators but they were still inferior in law.

● Below them were the *plebs*, the ordinary people, mainly poor, although still Roman citizens. Alongside them were *liberti*, or freed slaves.

**SOURCE 5**
Statue of a Roman orator speaking in court.

## 2. A fair trial?

The law-courts had to recognise the legal distinctions between orders, but there were other problems too.

**(a) 'Orators'.** Cases could take ages to get to court and then take a long time to be heard. In important cases orators (something like our barristers) were employed to speak for a client (Source 5). Some simply inflated their fee by talking for hours (Source 6). Some orators hired gangs of spectators to applaud their speeches.

**(b) Bribery.** Juries could be bribed. As they were so large, this could be expensive. One lawyer, Hortensius, issued different-coloured voting cards to those jurors he had bribed, to make sure he got his money's worth.

**(c)** Some **jurors** were reluctant to carry out their civic duties. Source 7 describes some who would clearly rather be doing something else.

**(d) Punishments** were often harsh: whipping, exile, beating, death in the Games, crucifixion, death by hanging. Another is shown in Source 8.

### SOURCE 6

*Time in court was measured by using water-clocks. These were containers which emptied slowly, taking about 20 minutes each. Martial, a Roman writer, complains about a windbag in court:*

Seven water-clocks you asked for, Caecilianus, in loud tones, and the judge unwillingly granted them. But you speak much and long, with your head tilted back, swilling water out of a flask. I wish you would sate your thirst and your oratory by drinking out of your water-clock.

### SOURCE 7

They arrive just in time to escape a fine for absence and being gorged with wine they fill the urinals in the alleys on the way to court. On arrival, they gloomily bid the proceedings to begin. The parties state their case, the judge calls the witnesses and goes to pass water again. He returns, calls for written evidence, though he can hardly keep his eyes open for the wine he has drunk. They retire to consider their verdict and say: 'Why should we bother with these silly people? Aren't we better employed drinking Greek wine and eating fat thrushes?'

*Gaius Titius wrote about the magistrates who arrived in court straight from drinking and gambling.*

### SOURCE 8

Sometimes the death penalty was carried out by throwing the guilty person off this cliff – the Tarpeian Rock in Rome – as shown in this 19th-century drawing.

❖ *Any system probably works less well in practice than it is supposed to. Use the sources here to say whether you agree with this opinion of Roman justice.*

❖ *Do you think Roman justice was fair?*

### The legacy of Roman Law

Roman Law was continually growing, as magistrates reached judgements on new cases (see Principle 3 on page 12). Writers performed a useful task in collecting these judgements together. In the 2nd century AD Ulpian wrote such a collection. Most famous of all, in AD 528, after the capital of the Empire had moved to Constantinople, was the Code of Justinian. This code took the 100 or so existing volumes of Roman Law and summarised them in only six.

In reviewing past cases, writers tried to get behind the particular details of the case to find legal principles. Similarly, because the Empire embraced many lands, each with their own legal customs, Roman legal writers had to learn to look for underlying principles.

The strength of Roman Law lies in these books and codes. They are written down and so can be consulted by everyone, including future generations. They have helped establish sensible, rational and acceptable law in many lands.

# THE MIDDLE AGES AD 500 – 1500

| | |
|---|---|
| 408 | last Roman army leaves Britain |
| **500** | |
| 563 | St Columba founds Christian community at Iona, Scotland |
| 570 | Birth of Mohammad |
| 597 | St Augustine converts King of Kent to Christianity |
| 663 | Synod of Whitby. England accepts Pope as Head of the Church |
| 688 | Laws of King Ine of Wessex |
| **750** | |
| 805 | Danes invade England |
| 878 | Danes defeated by King Alfred |
| 954 | England becomes a united country |
| **1000** | |
| 1066 | Norman conquest of England |
| 1166 | Assize of Clarendon |
| 1170 | Murder of Thomas Becket |
| 1215 | Magna Carta |
| **1250** / 1282 | English conquest of Wales |
| 1361 | JP's Act |
| 1455–87 | Wars of the Roses |
| **1500** | |

## The Anglo-Saxons

The first Anglo-Saxons came to England from Northern Europe as soldiers to fight for the Romans. When the Romans decided not to defend Britain any longer, the Anglo-Saxons took over and settled most of England by about AD 550. By about 700 there were seven reasonably stable kingdoms in England. Despite Danish attacks and invasion in the 9th century, Anglo-Saxon England was a united land by 954.

## The Norman conquest

In 1066 Duke William of Normandy invaded England, defeated the last Anglo-Saxon king, Harold, at the battle of Hastings, and took over the country. He rewarded his followers by giving them land taken from the Anglo-Saxons

## English medieval rulers

Although it changed over the centuries, English monarchy was a feudal monarchy. Energetic and forceful rulers could make the system work well, but other kings faced rebellion, even deposition.

## The Church

England was re-converted to Christianity in the 7th century by monks from Ireland and from Rome. In 663, at the Synod of Whitby, English Christians agreed to join the Roman Catholic Church, accepting the Pope as head. The Church was an immensely powerful organisation, with huge lands and control over all learning and education.

## England, Wales, Ireland and Scotland

Some Norman lords carved out lands for themselves on the Welsh borders and in South Wales in the 11th century and in Ireland in the 12th century. Wales was completely conquered by Edward I in 1282; Scotland resisted and remained an independent kingdom to the end of the period.

## The people

The population of England rose to about 3 million by 1500, despite the setback of the Black Death in 1347–1349, which killed about one-third of the population. Most people worked on the land. They were poor but able to subsist in all but very bad years. By the later Middle Ages, an increase in trade led to the growth of several towns.

# ANGLO-SAXON LAW AND ORDER

## KEY QUESTIONS
◆ *How did law and order change over the Anglo-Saxon period?*
◆ *Was Anglo-Saxon law fair?*

## Invaders and settlers

The Anglo-Saxons came to Britain as invaders and settlers, from the 5th century onwards. Roman peace and order was shattered (Source 1). Christianity was driven out. Rival leaders squabbled for power. As the timechart on page 16 shows, this lasted until the late 7th century.

In these centuries there was hardly such a thing as a 'system' of law and order. If you were powerful enough, you got your own way. Early Anglo-Saxons had the custom of the **blood-feud**: this meant that you and your family had the right to take revenge on, even to kill, the person who had wronged you or any of his family.

During the 7th century England became a Christian country again. The Anglo-Saxons' faith was very strong and the Church flourished. Its literature, knowledge, learning and art became famous across Europe (Source 2). Also, by about 700, stable government returned, with England divided into seven kingdoms. This allowed Anglo-Saxon kings to devise a better system of law and order.

There were slightly different laws in each region, especially in the Danelaw, the area settled by the Danes and Vikings in the 9th century. Here there were many more freemen than in Anglo-Saxon society, where a majority were either slaves or unfree peasants.

Anglo-Saxon kings gave their laws three main features:

● They tried to improve on simple revenge-taking.

● They based law enforcement on the local community.

● When the community could not decide, they relied on God to make a judgement.

### SOURCE 2

Page from the 'Lindisfarne Gospel', made in 689 by Eadfrith, a monk at Lindisfarne, in honour of St Cuthbert.

### SOURCE 1

Swords glinted all around. In the middle of the towns there were bits of corpses covered with a purple crust of dried blood. A number of wretched survivors were caught and butchered.

*The Anglo-Saxon conquest of Britain, as described by a Romano-British monk, Gildas, in the 6th century.*

### SOURCE 3

In preparation for trial by ordeal, the priest said this to the accused:

I charge you by the Father and the Son and the Holy Ghost and by our Christianity which you have received, and by the Holy Cross on which God suffered, and by the Holy Gospel and by the relics which are in this church, that you should not dare partake of this sacrament nor go to the altar if you did this of which you are accused, or know who did it.

## Wergeld

The blood-feud was replaced by a system of payments made by the accused to the wronged person. These payments, called **wergeld** in case of death, and **botgeld** in case of injury, did not treat people equally. Thus the wergeld for a great noble was 1,200 shillings, a lesser noble, 600 shillings, a **ceorl** (peasant), 200 shillings and a slave 60 shillings (paid to the former slave's owner). The botgeld for a broken little finger was 1 shilling, a back tooth cost 4 shillings, and so on, with more if the sufferer was of a higher rank.

## Local justice

Kings held their own court, called the **witan**. By 1000 England had been divided up into **shires** each with a royal official, called a shire-reeve, or **sheriff**, who held his own court. Each shire was divided into **hundreds** (usually a hundred peasant farms). The hundred court met each month and every free man had to attend.

For law enforcement and crime prevention, every free male over 12 also had to belong to a group of ten people called the **tithing**. If an offence was committed by one of the tithing, the others had to get the accused to court or pay a fine. If one of the tithing was robbed, the whole tithing had to chase the offender and alert every other tithing in the hundred by raising the **hue and cry**.

The unfree could only seek justice in their lord's court.

## Trials

There were two procedures for trials, the first relying on the community, the second turning to God for the verdict.

At the court, the accused was usually told to bring a certain number of 'oath-helpers', or **compurgators**, to the next meeting. These were people who would swear that the accused was innocent. The number depended on the seriousness of the crime. In the close-knit communities, all of whom believed in the seriousness of oath-taking, the result was usually reliable, or at least accepted.

If compurgation failed, the accused faced **trial by ordeal**. In each type of ordeal the religious importance of what was happening was emphasised. The accused had to fast for three days, and take communion, where the priest gave him a fearsome warning (Source 3). The ordeals took place in church or near it, the priest was always present and usually administered the ordeal, which was called 'the judgement of God'.

- **Ordeal by hot water.** The accused had to put his/her hand (whole arm for more serious offences) into a tub of boiling water. The hand or arm was then bound up and examined after three days. If there was no sign of the wound festering, the person was innocent.

- **Ordeal by fire.** The accused had to pick up a red-hot iron weight of one pound and walk three paces with it. Again the hand was bound up, with the same test for innocence. An alternative was to make the accused walk across three red-hot ploughshares.

- **Ordeal by cold water.** (This ordeal was normally only used for slaves.) The accused was bound with hands behind bent knees, so that he/she could not swim, and lowered into the water. A knot had been tied in the rope 'the length of the accused's hair' from the body. If the accused sank until the knot was under water, the water was 'accepting' the person, and so he/she was innocent. If the person floated, the water was 'rejecting' the accused and he/she was guilty.

- Clerics could take the **ordeal by sacrament**. The accused ate the blessed bread and was guilty if he choked on it.

## Punishments

Punishments were intended to fit the crime. For example, murderers were hanged and those guilty of slander had their tongues cut out. Indeed, mutilation was quite common, with criminals losing an ear, hand, foot or nose (Source 4). The death penalty was not often used and, as was to be the case right up to the late 19th century, imprisonment was rare.

### SOURCE 4

If a commoner has often been accused of theft and is at last proved guilty his hand or foot shall be struck off.

*Law of King Ine, king of Wessex from about 688.*

❖ *Why do you think Anglo-Saxon rulers tried to involve the local community in law enforcement?*
❖ *Could we use the system of*
   *(i) tithing or*
   *(ii) oath-helpers today?*
   *What would be the problems?*
❖ *Would there be any benefits?*
❖ *Why would the system of trials by ordeal not be acceptable today?*

# THE GROWTH OF ROYAL JUSTICE

KEY QUESTIONS

**KEY QUESTIONS**
- ◆ *Did the Norman Conquest bring great changes in the law?*
- ◆ *What was royal justice?*
- ◆ *Why did medieval kings try to extend it all over the country?*

Source 1 shows that William the Conqueror brought both change and continuity to the laws of England. Judge for yourself which was more important.

Many things did not change. The entire local legal system, with sheriffs in each shire (called counties by the Normans), hundreds, tithings, hue and cry, oath-helpers and trial by ordeal continued unchanged. In this, William was only being realistic: local law enforcement was carried out by the local community. It was based on their laws and customs and what they thought was right. William's 5,000 Normans could hardly change the minds and attitudes of 1,500,000 English.

## SOURCE 1

I command that all shall obey the laws of King Edward*, with the addition of those decrees I have ordained for the welfare of the English people.

(*King Edward – Edward the Confessor – was king of England from 1042 to 1066. William claimed that Harold took the throne illegally, so Edward was William's predecessor.)
*From the Laws of William the Conqueror.*

## SOURCE 2

Trial by battle. Note that, as in all ordeals, God was being asked to decide who was guilty, as, they believed, He decided the results of all battles.

However, William did make several changes to the laws of England:

● **Forest laws**. William loved deer-hunting and declared several areas, amounting to nearly one-third of the country, to be protected forests. In these areas, special laws, the Forest Laws, applied. (For more on the Forest Laws, see page 29.)

● **Trial by battle**. The war-like Normans were used to this custom and wanted to continue it in England (Source 2). As before any ordeal, both contestants had to fast and pray. They fought with identical weapons, or with bare hands and with their teeth, until one called 'craven', meaning he gave in. He was then hanged.

● **Church courts** were established, see page 22.

● **Norman-French** became the language of court procedures and Latin the language of court records. This lasted until Oliver Cromwell made changes in the 17th century.

## Royal justice

The biggest problem for medieval English government, law and order was the 'over-mighty subject'. That is some barons, sheriffs and others became so powerful that they ignored court decisions and did what they liked (for more on this in the later Middle Ages, see pages 29–31). A particularly bad period of this type of lawlessness was in 1135 to 1154, just before Henry II came to the throne.

## Henry II (1154–1189)

The Anglo-Saxons had a concept called the 'peace'. Everyone was entitled to peace in and around their home. Especially powerful was the 'King's Peace', which surrounded him wherever he went and also covered the main roads (hence 'The King's Highway'), women, Jews and foreigners. Crimes committed within the King's Peace were treated more severely.

Henry extended this idea of the King's Peace to cover the whole kingdom. At the Assize of Clarendon in 1166 (an assize is a sitting of the king's court, from the French, *assoir* = to sit) he brought in a number of changes. Many were repeated and revised by the Assize of Northampton, 1176.

## SOURCE 3

Medieval illustration of judges and prisoners.

## SOURCE 4

King Henry, on the advice of all his barons, for the preservation of peace and the maintenance of justice, has decreed that enquiry shall be made through all the counties and hundreds, through twelve men of the hundred, upon oath that they will speak the truth, whether there be in their hundred, any man accused or suspect of being a robber or murderer.

And in every county where there is no gaol, let such be made in a borough or some castle of the king, at the king's expense and from his wood.

*From the Assize of Clarendon, 1166.*

● **Travelling justices**, called 'justices in eyre'. Following the king around to get him to hear your case could take years and cost you a fortune. Justices in eyre had been started by Henry I but Henry II got the system going again. They were royal judges, sent into the country to hear cases (Source 3). So great was the demand in civil cases (disputes between people, usually over land, not involving crime), that a permanent court was set up at Westminster in 1178 to deal with them.

● **Juries of presentment** were set up (Source 4). In these juries 12 local people had to report, on oath, any serious breaches of the law, to the justices or the sheriff. Juries too had been used before, for example in the Domesday Book enquiry, but Henry made them a regular and important part of the legal process. Note that this 'Grand Jury', as it was called, did not decide the case – this was still done by ordeal – but was used to bring suspects to trial.

● **County gaols** were built (Source 4).

● In some civil cases people could choose to have their case decided by a jury. They could buy a 'writ' from the king ordering the case to be tried by jury in the king's court rather than in the (possibly corrupt) baron's court.

These extensions of royal justice continued under Henry's successors. In 1194 county coroners were set up. They had to enquire into any sudden or unusual deaths and also deal with people in sanctuary (see page 23). The system of trial by jury increased, especially after trials by ordeal ended in 1215 when the Church refused to take part in them. It was then called a 'petty jury', to distinguish it from the grand jury. From the 14th century decisions had to be unanimous. Royal writs increased in number and popularity: in 1216 there were about 60 kinds of writs; by 1320 there were 890.

Royal justice thus achieved two things: it brought quicker, fairer justice to the people of England, and it made money for the king by selling writs and collecting fines.

### Origins of the Justices of the Peace (JPs)

In the later Middle Ages the gentry, people ranking below the barons, became involved in helping to administer local justice. In 1361 the Justices of the Peace Act appointed three or four JPs per county, with power to fine, arrest and bind people over to keep the peace. They were allowed 4/-(20p) per day expenses. By the 15th century there were up to 20 per county. They heard juries of presentment at county level and held their own courts four times a year – the Quarter Sessions. They were ready for their hey-day under the Tudors, see page 37.

❖ *Was continuity or change in the law and the legal system more important following the Norman Conquest?*

❖ *Why was royal justice successful?*
*List your reasons. Develop each one into a short paragraph, describing the problem and the solution royal justice offered.*

# LAW AND ORDER AND THE CHURCH

## KEY QUESTION

◆ *Was the Church an obstacle to good law and order?*

We have already seen that religious beliefs had a powerful influence on the law, through trial by ordeal and the importance of oaths. How else did the Church influence law and order?

## Benefit of clergy

The Church claimed the right to try any churchman accused of a crime in its own courts. This was called **benefit of clergy** and dated from the time when ordinary courts offered rough justice which the Church did not trust. It was intended just to cover priests, but soon anyone loosely connected with the Church claimed it, even people like church doorkeepers.

Courts tried to find some proof of church membership. Having a tonsure – the special priest's haircut – was used, but anyone can cut their hair. Then a reading test was used, as priests were almost the only educated people, but soon anyone who could read was allowed to claim benefit of clergy.

**SOURCE 1**
Thomas Becket and Henry II – a stained-glass window from Canterbury Cathedral.

### SOURCE 2

• Hamo Corbyl is cited for adultery with Basilea Forne and though he has often been corrected, he does not fear to repeat the offence. An inquest was held and they were both found guilty. He also behaves badly towards his wife. She appeared and they were reconciled. They agree to live together under pain of seven floggings in the neighbouring markets. Hamo and Basilea were also flogged five times round Romney market and five times through Hythe market and six times around their parish church.

• The chaplain of Norrington has much land and busies himself too much with secular affairs.

• Elias, a clerk (a priest), keeps a certain Agatha in his house for immoral purposes. He is to be flogged three times round his church.

• The vicar of Aldington quarrels with his parishioners and knows not how to carry on a discussion without flying into a great rage.

• Alexander Overy does not attend his parish church as he is bound to do. He confesses the charge and swears that he will come in future.

*Offences brought before the Archbishop of Canterbury's court between 1292 and 1328.*

This annoyed kings who were trying to establish royal justice, especially Henry II (see page 21). He was displeased partly because people who were not really clerics were escaping his courts, but mainly because he thought criminals were getting off more lightly in Church courts which could not sentence someone to death. This brought him into conflict with his old friend, Thomas Becket, whom Henry had made Archbishop of Canterbury (Source 1). Eventually four of Henry's knights murdered Becket in Canterbury Cathedral in 1170. It is a sign of the Church's power that Henry was forced to seek a humiliating forgiveness, lying barefoot on the floor in front of Becket's tomb while bishops, abbots and the monks of Canterbury beat him. Benefit of clergy remained; it was not abolished until the 1820s.

Church courts dealt with all kinds of matters. Many of them dealt with sexual offences, but by no means all. In Essex in the early

Sanctuary knocker from Durham Cathedral.

16th century, clergy were had up for incompetence, bad behaviour, sheltering sheep in the church; other men and women were had up for telling tales, fighting during the sermon, dancing on Sundays, witchcraft, vandalism, drunkenness and playing football during service-time. You can use Source 2 to read some actual examples. You can then decide for yourself if Henry was right that they let you off lightly.

********** PUNISHMENT BOX***********

### Shaming punishments

The Church courts used shaming punishments, such as public penance, and local courts used the stocks or the pillory. The purpose of these punishments was to shame the offender in front of his or her neighbours.

*************************************

## Sanctuary

If someone on the run from the law got to a church, he or she could not be arrested. At Durham, Beverley and the Abbeys of Westminster, Glastonbury and Beaulieu, this right of sanctuary extended for a mile around the church. Someone who grasped the knocker at Durham Cathedral (Source 3) was especially safe.

You then had to throw yourself on the mercy of the Church. At Beverley you had to be 'faithful and true to the Archbishop of York, bear good heart to the bailiff, government, burgesses and citizens of Beverley, never carry weapons, be ready for strife or fire, ring the bells and attend Mass.'

On 24 May 1379, William Palmer, who was outlawed for the death of Thomas Wydenhale was arrested and put in the stocks. But he broke them and fled to Leighton Buzzard church and stayed there for 13 days. On 6 June he confessed to William Fancott, county coroner, that he had murdered Thomas on 5 June 1370. He sought the liberty of the Church and it was granted to him. On the same day, before the coroner, at the church gate, he was given the port of Dover, chose his route and abjured the realm of England.

*A coroner describes how a murderer who has sought sanctuary was dealt with.*

After a while the county coroner would hear your case. If you confessed, as in Source 4, you were allowed to 'abjure' (swear to leave) the country. You were given a port to leave by and a route to follow. Wearing sackcloth, barefoot, bare-headed, branded with an 'A' (for abjured) on the thumb, you made your way, in a given time and under escort, to the port. You had to catch the next boat, or, if there wasn't one, wade out into the sea each day until one was ready.

## What kinds of people claimed sanctuary?

Traitors, heretics, sorcerers, outlaws, clerics and those with a criminal record could not claim sanctuary. Out of 243 sanctuary-seekers at Durham between 1464 and 1524, there were 195 murderers, 16 debtors, 9 cattle-stealers, 7 thieves, 4 prison escapees, 4 housebreakers and 8 others. The Church saw sanctuary as a refuge from the brutality or unfairness of the secular law. The right soon lapsed under the Tudors: Henry VII excluded debtors from claiming the right. Henry VIII excluded those accused of rape, murder, burglary and arson. The Dissolution of the Monasteries and the Reformation put an end to it completely.

❖ *The Church believed that the real judgement on your life came when you died. They saw their role as offering mercy to those accused of crimes. How might a king who was concerned with justice reply to these beliefs?*
❖ *Was the Church's influence on the law for good or bad?*
❖ *Use this table to list points on each side of the argument. Then write up your answer in six short paragraphs.*

|  | GOOD | BAD |
| --- | --- | --- |
| Ordeal |  |  |
| Benefit of clergy |  |  |
| Sanctuary |  |  |

# THE MANOR COURT

## KEY QUESTIONS
◆ *How did the law control people's lives in the Middle Ages?*
◆ *Did ordinary people feel safe from crime in the Middle Ages?*

Most people in medieval England lived in villages. Their lives were much more closely bound up with each other than we are with our neighbours today.

They farmed the land in strips that were mixed up together, so that they had to co-operate in everyday farming jobs. This work was directed by the **reeve** (Source 1), who was elected from among the villagers. Many of the villagers were **villeins**, that is, they were closely tied to their lord or lady, to whom they owed all sorts of feudal dues. Some of these are shown in Source 2. Others included not being allowed to marry, travel or trade without your lord's or lady's consent.

What happened if something went wrong in this complicated network of things you were supposed to do?

## SOURCE 1
A reeve giving instructions to the villagers.

## SOURCE 2

Each villein is to work for two days a week for the lord. He provides the lord with a horse for one journey a year. He must bring one cartload of wood. At Christmas he must provide two hens and a barrel of malt.

*Some of the feudal duties to be carried out by villeins at Burton-on-Trent.*

## SOURCE 3A

(1) Fined: Richard de Bothen, for grinding corn elsewhere than in the Earl's [the Earl of Lincoln's] mill.

(2) Juliana, wife of Richard Pykard, brewed ale illegally. When the ale-tasters came, Juliana said she would sell ale against their will. She is fined 12d (5p).

(3) A jury is summoned to inquire into the case of Hancock le Nunne's sheep. His wife Alicia is in mercy [accused] of saying that the jury were all perjured [swearing something untrue] and Adam Gerbot would perjure himself for a gallon of ale.

(4) William Jordan is in mercy for bad ploughing. Fined 6d (2.5p)

(5) Bete, widow of Robert Heget, commonly curses her neighbours and makes an outcry in the town at night. She also raised the hue and cry against Richard Cay unjustly.

(6) Rayner the chaplain complains of Susannah de Brighouse that she insulted him, calling him a lazy little man.

*Extracts from the court rolls of Wakefield in 1294. (The 'rolls' are the records of the court's decisions.)*

## SOURCE 3B

(7) William, son of Richard Cook, gives the lord 2/- (10p) for license to cultivate the lands of villeins whenever they are unfit to cultivate their own land.

(8) Richard de Putteway, being old and infirm, gives back all his land in return for which the lord gives him a loaf of brown bread and 3 gallons of beer a week, regular meals with the free servants of the Abbey and 5/-(25p) a year to clothe himself.

(9) Philip Gerard returns into the lord's hands 10 strips of land, of which 6 lie on one side and 4 on the other side of the strips of John Walters in the field named Arnley.

*From the court rolls of the Manor of Halesowen, 1294.*

## The manor court

Every lord or lady held a manor court every three or four weeks at which all these little disputes touching people's daily lives were settled. Anyone who owed any service to the lord or lady had to attend. Many manor courts were also Courts Leet, and could deal with minor criminal offences too. The reeve described what offence had been committed and the lord or lady passed judgement. Source 3 shows the wide range of issues dealt with at manor courts, such as farming, housing, family disputes and village squabbles. The court also elected all kinds of local officials such as the ale-taster and the village constable.

**SOURCE 5**

A villein carries a sack of corn to his lord's mill, early 14th century. The villagers often had to have their corn ground in their lord's mill, a rule which they resented as the lord would take a cut for doing the work – see also Source 3A.

**SOURCE 4**

(11) Isabella Porter should come to court to reply to Matilda Alured on a charge of keeping a sow which killed and ate 14 ducklings belonging to the said Matilda.

(12) Henry Derex is accused of being found with a long knife after the great bell, against the custom of the town*.

(13) John Knight and Rose his wife, being lepers, roam in the market-place, selling and buying food, especially geese and chickens. They are accustomed to embrace and kiss children, whereby they may, as many think, catch the leprosy. Their removal is demanded.

(14) Richard Careman accuses John Wulf of violent assault in St. John's Field. John stole several books from him, which he then threw in a ditch.

(15) Hugh van der Meer, Clays van der Meer and Geoffrey Maire, being Flemings, have undertaken not to draw knife or sword in Colchester, according to an ordinance made to that effect with the consent of all Flemings. They now pay fines for breaking that order.

(16) John Kentysh is accused of keeping certain articles of clothing lent by William Baroun, that is: a death's head mask, a suit with tails, etc. for a play, which Kentysh undertook to return once the play was finished.

*In Colchester, as in many towns, a great bell, the curfew bell, was tolled at nightfall and it was an offence to carry a weapon or be out after this without good cause.*

*Extracts from the court rolls of the town of Colchester in 1310.*

## Towns

During the Middle Ages, towns in England grew in number and size. To establish a town, you needed a charter from the king. One of the rights the charter gave was freedom from the local manor court and the right to hold a borough court. Source 4 shows the kinds of things the borough court of the town of Colchester was dealing with.

❖ *Look at the 16 offences from the court rolls given in Sources 3 and 4. Use this table to sort them:*

| Land and farming | Other dues owed to the lord | Crimes | Un-neighbourly behaviour |
|---|---|---|---|
| | | | |

❖ *Suggest punishments for each of the 16 offences here.*
❖ *Which do you regard as the most serious offence listed here?*
❖ *Which kinds of offences can be found in the court rolls of Colchester (Source 4), which you would probably NOT find in a village court?*
❖ *Which of the 16 offences here would not appear in court today? Is this because they are:*
*(i) no longer offences?*
*(ii) too unimportant?*
❖ *'Medieval villagers and townsfolk did not suffer from crime because the whole community was involved in dealing with it.'*
*Is this an accurate interpretation of their lives, based on the evidence here?*

# WOMEN AND THE LAW

## KEY QUESTION

◆ *What did the law say about the position of women in medieval times?*

The law reflects the way people – usually men– think things ought to be. In medieval times, men expected women to behave in certain ways: for example, there was a special offence for women whom neighbours called a 'scold' (see Source 1). The ducking-stool (Source 2) was used in some places for women who broke this code of behaviour.

The Church taught that women were inferior (Source 3), and most people agreed. Women were paid less for the same work: for hay-making, for example, a man was paid 12d (5p) a day, and a woman 8d (3p). Many jobs were closed to a woman: she could not go to university, travel on her own, become a doctor, a lawyer or a priest, join the army or become an MP.

## SOURCE 1

Alice Shether was brought before the Mayor for being a common scold. All her neighbours were greatly molested and annoyed by her malicious words and abuse. She sowed envy among them, discord and ill-will, repeatedly defaming and backbiting many of them.

*Alice asked for trial by jury, was found guilty and sentenced to an hour in the pillory. From the city records of London, 1375.*

## SOURCE 2

A 13th-century picture of a ducking-stool.

A woman had to obey her father when she was living at home and then obey her husband when she married. Norman law was much harder on women than Anglo-Saxon law. A woman, such as the one shown getting married in Source 4, had very few rights of her own:

● She could not own any property, not even clothes or jewellery. This meant she could not run her own business, or trade. Everything she had belonged to her husband.

● Because of this, her parents would not let her marry without their agreement.

● She could not divorce her husband.

● If he divorced her, she would not get custody of their children.

● If the couple had sons and daughters, only the sons would inherit anything when the father died.

● Only widows had some right to own property – the 'dower', land or goods specially set aside for her support in her lifetime (see Source 5).

## The records of the law courts

A major problem in trying to find out about women's lives in medieval times is the lack of evidence. Few women could write and the history of kings, battles, parliaments and rebellions is almost entirely male history. Court records help to fill this gap, especially the records of local manorial courts – the court rolls. As we saw on pages 24 and 25, they record the minor squabbles and problems in the everyday lives of ordinary people. The picture of women's lives which we find in these is not quite what you would expect.

## SOURCE 3

Women's authority is nil; let her in all things be subject to the rule of men. Neither can she teach, nor be a witness in court, nor sit in judgement.

*Gratian, an 11th-century Church lawyer, comments on the position of women.*

## SOURCE 4

A medieval wedding.

## SOURCE 5

A widow shall have as her dower* up to one-third of the inheritance . . . She shall also have her dowry*, as much as was given to her on her betrothal.

If the dower or dowry is denied to the widow, it shall be restored on the oath of the men who were present at her betrothal.

**Dower:** *Goods or land, usually one-third of his property, given by a husband to his wife on their marriage. This was to support her if she was widowed. On her death the dower returned to her husband's heirs.*

**Dowry:** *Property given by a father to a women's future husband when they got married.*

*Norman Laws of the early 13th century.*

## SOURCE 6A

Constance, daughter of Roger de London, complains that the same Roger unjustly sold for 9/- (45p) a cow given to his three daughters. She seeks her share and Roger is fined 3/- (15p).

*From the Court Rolls of Chalgrave Manor, 1278.*

## SOURCE 6B

William of Stansgate met the widow Desiderata, a particular friend and godmother of his son. She asked him in jest if he was one of the men appointed by the king to keep the peace. She declared she could overcome two or three men like him, crooked her leg, grabbed him by the neck and threw him to the ground.

*From a medieval Court roll, 1267.*

❖ *Look back over all the cases referred to on pages 24 and 25, Sources 3A, 3B and 4. Look also at the cases in the Church Courts, page 22, Source 2, and at Source 6 (above).*
  – *How many cases involved women?*
  – *Are women involved as accuser, or accused?*
  – *Do the courts seem open to women seeking justice?*
  – *What picture of medieval women do you get from these court records?*

# ROBIN HOOD

*KEY QUESTION*
◆ *Why has the story of Robin Hood been so popular for so long?*

The story of Robin Hood, the outlaw who robbed the rich to give to the poor, has been popular for centuries. Look at Sources 1 to 4. Whatever the popular means of entertainment, there has been a version of his story. Source 1 publicises just one of the most recent of many film and television Robin Hoods. Source 2 is from a 19th-century children's book. Similar books exist for the 18th, 17th and 16th centuries. Before printing was invented, stories were often told in verses, called ballads, because the rhyme and rhythm made them easier to remember. The first printers put popular ballads from the time into their books. 'A Mery Geste of Robyn Hoode' was first published in 1492; Source 3 is from an edition of 1510.

Before about 1500 there are only second-hand references to Robin Hood, but his story was obviously popular entertainment. In 1473 Sir John Paston mentioned in a letter that a man was to appear in a play called 'Robyn Hod and the Shryff of Nottyngham'. Source 4 suggests that there was a popular rhyme about Robin Hood in the late 14th century, and that seems to be as far back as we can go.

**SOURCE 1**

From Kevin Costner's film, 'Robin Hood'. There have been at least 14 Robin Hood films, the first in 1922, including a cartoon version, and at least two TV series.

## Was there a real Robin Hood?

According to the stories, Robin Hood was the true heir of the Earl of Huntingdon, born at Locksley and robbed of his inheritance by Prince John, King Richard I's brother, while Richard was away on a Crusade. Richard was king from 1189 to 1199, but was indeed away from England for most of the 1190s. Some parts of the story do not quite fit these dates. For example, Friar Tuck: there were no friars in England until the 1220s. There is a place called Loxley, near Sheffield, about 20 miles from Sherwood Forest. We therefore have a rough time and place for the real Robin Hood.

However, any attempt by historians to find an outlaw called Robin Hood who did anything like the things the storybook Robin Hood is supposed to have done have failed. The best that can be found is one 'Robert Hode' running away to be an outlaw in West Yorkshire in 1225.

## Why has Robin Hood been such a popular hero?

Perhaps there was a real Robin (or Robert) Hood who had to become an outlaw. What seems to have happened is that the other episodes and characters in the story have been added on over the years. What is clear, however, is that the whole story was very popular by the later Middle Ages. Why should someone who had broken the law, and was a robber and trickster, be so popular? What does this tell us about people of that time?

● He was an **outlaw**. In the Middle Ages, someone who was accused of a crime, but failed to turn up in court to answer the charge, was declared an outlaw. This meant he or she lost all the protection of the law, and all their rights to own property. Remember that there was no police force to chase criminals and that there were plenty of wild places, like forests, to hide. But, as we have seen, the law could be used by powerful people to get what they wanted. Many people could sympathise with Robin Hood's suffering from unfair court decisions.

● Robin and his father, the Earl of Huntingdon, were Saxons; John was a Norman. The savage conquest of England by the Normans in the years after 1066 was not forgotten, especially in the north, which was brutally laid waste by William the Conqueror in 1069–1070.

## SOURCE 2

Illustration from a storybook about Robin Hood published in 1850.

## SOURCE 3

Two verses and title-page illustration from 'A Mery Geste of Robyn Hoode' published in 1510:

Give ear and listen gentlemen

That be of free-born blood:

I shall you tell of a good yeoman

His name was Robin Hood

Robin was a proud outlaw,

While he walked on the ground,

So courteous an outlaw as he was one

Was never none else found.

## SOURCE 4

*In about 1377 William Langland described a character in a poem he was writing called Sloth:*

I cannot perfectly say the Lord's Prayer as the priest sings it, but I know the rhyme of Robin Hood.

● John fits into the story as the mythical 'bad King John'; every good story has its villains as well as its heroes.

● Another villain is Guy of Gisborne. He is a typical example of the 'over-mighty subject', the main threat to law and order in the Middle Ages. Many ordinary people failed to get justice because powerful lords intervened in the law.

● The arch-villain is the Sheriff of Nottingham. The sheriff was the chief royal official in every county. Many were corrupt and misused their powers. No wonder the Sheriff of Nottingham was the man they loved to hate!

● There are other victims of Robin and his outlaws. Many were just the kinds of people who were widely disliked in medieval times: rich abbots, crooked traders, greedy Norman landowners.

● Robin Hood and his merry men lived by shooting deer in the forest. The Normans loved deer-hunting.

After the Norman Conquest large areas of England were declared Royal Forests. These areas were subject to special laws called the Forest Laws. The laws were very strict. Not only were you not allowed to kill deer but also you could not carry a bow, or cut timber, or clear the land to grow crops. If you owned a dog, it had to have its paws clipped so that it could not run. The punishments for breaking the Forest Laws were ferocious. Not surprisingly, these laws were widely resented and listeners must have experienced a shiver of glee as they heard the story-teller describe Robin getting away with killing another deer and feasting on the venison.

● He robbed the rich to give to the poor. Who can disagree with that? Popular heroes who robbed the rich to give to the poor are not confined to Britain. The Australian outlaw Ned Kelly was hanged in 1880; within a few years of his death he was the hero of popular songs and ballads, giving him Robin Hood-like qualities. In the USA outlaws like Billy the Kid (real name William Bonney, shot by Sheriff Pat Garrett in 1881, aged 21) and Jesse James were talked of in the same way as Robin Hood.

❖ *What does the popularity of the story of Robin Hood tell us about people's feelings about the law in medieval England? Use the eight points above to answer this question. Write a sentence about each of them.*
❖ *Why is the story of Robin Hood still popular today?*

# THE OVER-MIGHTY SUBJECT

*KEY QUESTION*
◆ *Why did law and order break down in the later Middle Ages?*

The medieval system of justice worked fairly well in the 11th, 12th and 13th centuries. Under a vigorous monarch, such as Henry II (see page 21), people did their jobs and the law was enforced. Even so, under an unpopular monarch, like King John who reigned from 1199 to 1216, the system broke down (see Sources 1 and 2). We should be careful not to rely too much on Source 1, because John quarrelled with the Church, and the artist was a monk. However, Magna Carta, the great charter which his enemies forced John to sign in 1215, lists providing justice among the things they expected him to do (Source 2). You can easily work out from these two clauses what had gone wrong with justice in his reign.

Source 3 shows how far people were taking the law into their own hands by the 15th century. Incidents like this were quite common. Why?

## The personality of the king

How far the laws and the powers of the courts were observed depended too much on the personality of the king. Only he had the authority to make sure it worked. Some kings did personally sit in judgement. Richard II went in person to St Albans in 1381 to preside over the trial of John Ball, leader of the Peasants' Revolt. Henry V sat in court at Lichfield for two months in 1414 dealing with religious rebels.

However, some kings, notably Edward II and Henry VI, were weak. Even strong kings were often away at war: Edward I was in France from 1286 to 1289; Edward III was continuously at war from 1335 to 1347.

## The over-mighty subject

If the rule of law is going to work, it has to be enforced, not only on the weak, but on the strong. In the 14th and 15th centuries there were too many powerful people who had no respect for the law. For example, in 1308, Sir Roger Swynnerton went to the county court at Stafford with a gang of followers. He put guards on the doors and prevented anyone from leaving until the court had returned the verdict he wanted. In 1332 the Folvilles, a Leicestershire gang, captured and ransomed a judge. In 1423 Sampson Meverel and a group of followers lay in wait for some jurors on their way to court and forced them to swear that they would declare him innocent.

## SOURCE 1

Brutality and injustice in the reign of King John, early 13th century.

## SOURCE 2

39. No free man shall be imprisoned, or stripped of his rights or possessions, or outlawed, nor will we proceed with force against him, except by the lawful judgement of his equals or by the law of the land.

40. To no one will we sell, deny or delay justice.

*Two clauses from Magna Carta, 1215.*

## SOURCE 3

Lord Moleyns sent against us a riotous people to the number of a thousand persons, dressed in manner of war, with bows, guns, long crooks to drag down houses, and long trees with which they broke up the gates and doors, and so came into the house where my wife was and twelve persons with her. The which twelve persons they drove out of the house and then they mined down the wall of the room where my wife was and drove her out of the gates. They cut the posts of the houses to let them fall and took all the stuff to the value of £200.

*Petition of John Paston to Parliament, 1449.*

Note that the law-breakers in these cases and in Source 3 were powerful lords, not peasants. This was the era of the 'over-mighty subject', people who had lands and followers, and who should have been subject to the king, but chose to disregard the law. One historian has called this 'fur-collar crime.' Two features of late medieval life contributed to this high level of crime:

● **Livery**. England was at war for most of the period from the late 13th to the late 15th century, with Wales, Scotland and France. Kings called on lords to provide them with soldiers, as they had to do. Lords equipped their men with their badge or uniform, called their **livery**. When there was a period of peace, these soldiers came home, with nothing to do. Many lords kept them on as their own private armies, still wearing their livery, terrorising local people and the local courts. Source 4 also describes what these gangs were like.

● **Maintenance.** Lords looked after their liveried followers, and they also **maintained** them. This meant feeding and clothing them but it also meant protecting them from the law, or ensuring they got off if they did come to court for doing the lord's dirty work.

The following incident, from 1385, shows how the custom of livery and maintenance could lead to trouble and how people who should have known better behaved: An archer wearing the livery of Ralph Stafford quarrelled with one of Sir John Holland's squires and killed him. Ralph Stafford rode out to meet Sir John Holland, who struck him down. The feud between the two powerful men and their followers went on for years, during which many ordinary people were injured.

## Weaknesses in the legal system

With weak or absent kings, the legal system was too weak to cope with over-mighty subjects.

● Officials were corrupt: sheriffs put their own followers on juries and took bribes. In the 1330s Chief Justice Wylughby was said to 'sell laws as if they were oxen or cows'.

● The system for catching law-breakers was weak. The tithing system and hue and cry depended on a stable society in which people knew each other's business. This was crumbling as people moved around more. In some courts as many as 80% of those named by a grand jury failed to appear.

● JPs (see page 21) were too weak to stand up to aristocrat criminals.

● Juries could be bullied or bribed. Ordinary people called as jurymen dared not stand up to local lords. Putting pressure on juries in this way was called 'embracery', and was common.

● Punishments did not deter. Many people were only fined or even pardoned. Despite the gallows in Source 5, hanging was rare.

### SOURCE 4

*John Bromyard, a friar, describes the lawlessness caused by livery and maintenance in the 15th century:*

No hounds were ever readier for the chase, no falcon hungrier for the bird it has spied, than are these to do whatever their great lords bid them, if he should want to beat, or spoil, or kill anyone.

### SOURCE 5

A justice in eyre in the 14th century, sentencing a prisoner to be hanged. The 'T'-shaped gallows is behind them.

❖ *Read Source 2. What had John been doing (or not doing) according to the authors of Magna Carta?*
❖ *Note Clause 39 in Source 2. What kind of trial can free men expect?*
  *(Note that this only applies to free men: Clause 39 did not give a general right to this kind of trial.)*
❖ *If you were an adviser to a new ruler, coming to the throne in the late 15th century, what advice would you give about improving law and order in England? Deal with all the points on this page in sequence. Then check with page 36 to see how close you were to what the Tudors actually did.*

# LAW AND ORDER IN THE WORLD OF ISLAM

*KEY QUESTIONS*
◆ *Who kept law and order in Muslim countries?*

The religion of Islam was founded by Muhammad. He was born about AD 570, in Mecca, in Arabia, and worked for many years as a merchant. He used to visit a cave in the mountains, where he was visited by an angel, who told him to write down a message from God. Over a period, Muhammad received many of these messages and spent the rest of his life telling people about them and encouraging them to follow God's commands. After his death, these messages were written down in the *Qur'an*.

When he died in 632 most of the people of Arabia were followers of Islam, called Muslims. By the mid-8th century Muslims had conquered enormous lands from central France in the west, across North Africa, the Middle East to Persia, central Asia and the borders of India.

## Holy law – Shari'ah

One of the things that united all these different people was the Holy Law, called **Shari'ah**, as written down in the *Qur'an* and in the sayings of Muhammad. Shari'ah was God's law, as revealed to His prophet Muhammad, so it governed the whole universe, for all time. Breaking the law therefore meant going against the

### SOURCE 3
Turkish Sultan Beyazid surrounded by his advisers. The *Qur'an* tells rulers: 'When you judge between people, exercise your judgement wisely'.

### SOURCE 1

(a) 'Liquor and gambling, idols and divining arrows are only a filthy work of Satan; give them up so that you may prosper.'

(b) 'As for the thief, both man and women, chop off their hands. It is the reward for their own deeds and exemplary punishment from God.'

*Laws from the* Qur'an.

### SOURCE 2

A man may be punished by having his face blackened and being paraded mounted backwards on an ass. It is related that 'Umar ibn al-Khattab, may God be pleased with him, used this punishment for a false witness. Because the liar blackened a reputation, his face was blackened; because he turned words backwards, he was mounted backwards.

*From a book on Islamic law by Ibn Taymiyya, written about 1311–1315.*

whole of creation and was a sin as well as a crime. Source 1(a), for example, groups together prohibition of alcohol, gambling and superstition. Shari'ah governed every aspect of life, with rules on diet, education, dress, marriage, family life, business, government, how to greet another person, hospitality – even the way to drink a glass of water. As Source 1(b) shows, it laid down specific punishments as well.

Under Shari'ah, a woman was expected to be obedient, first to her father, then to her husband; the *Qur'an* says: 'The men are a degree above them'. But the *Qur'an* also guarantees some women's rights: for example, to own property, take part in government and sue for divorce.

## New crimes

However detailed the Shari'ah may be, there are always new situations, new disputes, new crimes. Muslim lawyers divide all behaviour into five categories: forbidden, discouraged, neutral, recommended and compulsory. Someone who does what is forbidden, or will not do what is compulsory, has committed a crime. Settling disputes between people (civil law) is based on doing what is recommended and avoiding what is discouraged.

Rulers have a duty to see that the law is properly and fairly enforced (Source 3). But judgements are made by judges, known as **qadis** (Source 4). As Source 5

A qadi hearing a family dispute.

shows, a qadi has to have a deep knowledge of the *Qur'an* and the Shari'ah. Muslim history has many stories of qadis who successfully defied a Sultan or Caliph. For example, a 15th-century Turkish qadi, Al-Fanari, refused to allow the Sultan Beyezit to be a witness in his court because the Sultan was neglecting to attend daily prayers. The Sultan took note, and built the Beyezit Mosque.

## Punishments

Punishment is the judgement of Almighty God and is not intended to reform the criminal. It is based on the principle of 'an eye for an eye and a tooth for a tooth', as God revealed to Moses (who is also a prophet of Islam). Thus the punishment for murder is beheading, for theft is cutting off the right hand and for adultery is stoning to death.

It is important to understand that these harsh punishments were actually an improvement on how things were in Muhammad's lifetime. In his time feuds were common, and went on for years, sometimes for generations; revenge was often savage. These punishments are called **'Hadd'**, which means **limitation**: the community took its punishment on a thief by cutting off his hand, and that was the end of it. This was better than a long-drawn out revenge feud which had no limit.

### SOURCE 5

*The seven conditions to be a qadi, from a book on Islamic law by Al-Mawardi, written in the 11th century:*

1. He must be a man.
2. He must be intelligent.
3. He must be a free man.
4. He must be a Muslim.
5. He must be trustworthy and virtuous.
6. He must be sound of sight and hearing.
7. He must be learned in the rules of Holy Law.

The other thing to remember about hadd punishments is that the *Qur'an* says that they should be used rarely. Qadis more often reduced the punishment below the prescribed hadd and tried to find a punishment that fitted the crime (see Source 2).

❖ *Compare Islamic law with the laws of the ancient world (pages 10 to 11). What are the similiarities and differences?*
❖ *Which would you prefer to live under: law in England in the Middle Ages, or Islamic law? Give your reasons.*

# THE STORY 3
# EARLY MODERN BRITAIN 1500–1750

| | |
|---|---|
| 1450 | |
| 1485 | Henry VII: the first Tudor monarch |
| 1500 | |
| 1534 | Henry VIII becomes head of the Church |
| 1536 | Pilgrimage of Grace |
| 1549 | Kett's Rebellion |
| 1550 | |
| 1561 | JPs given powers to fix wages |
| 1600 | |
| 1601 | Poor Law |
| 1605 | Gunpowder Plot |
| 1642 | Start of Civil War |
| 1649 | Execution of Charles I |
| 1650 | |
| 1688 | Glorious Revolution |
| 1700 | |
| 1726 | Execution of Jonathan Wild |
| 1736 | Witchcraft ceases to be an offence |
| 1739 | Dick Turpin hanged |
| 1746 | Hawkhurst smuggler gang attack Poole Custom House |
| 1750 | |

## Monarchy

Henry VII (1485–1509) set up a strong monarchy for his Tudor family. It was strengthened by his son, Henry VIII (1509–1547), and by Henry VIII's daughter Elizabeth I (1558–1603).

## Religious conflict

The unity of religion in England of the Roman Catholic Church was broken when Henry VIII made himself Head of the Church in England. Henry soon started dissolving the monasteries. England's religion changed again under Mary I (1553–1558), and again when Elizabeth came to the throne. Those people who were at odds with the religious views and policies of the monarch were persecuted, sometimes killed.

## Civil War

Opposition to the policies of Charles I (1624–1649) led to a bloody and drawn-out Civil War. This ended with the defeat of Charles and his execution. There was then a republic. Radical and democratic ideas were widely discussed. One of the army leaders, Oliver Cromwell, ruled from 1652–1658, but the monarchy was restored in 1660.

## Glorious Revolution and Settlement

James II (1684–1688) offended the country by trying to restore Roman Catholicism and was driven out in 1688. William of Orange was invited to become King William III (1689–1701), ruling jointly with his wife, Mary II. However, the real winners of the 'Glorious Revolution' were the better-off property-owning classes: landowners, bankers and rich merchants.

## The people

The population rose throughout the 16th century, from 3 million to 5 million. Food prices rose sharply and real wages (what you can actually buy with your money) fell. This bad situation was made even worse during 1590–1640 by several bad harvests. Population pressure eased off in the later 17th and early 18th centuries. Harvests were better. The country prospered, with steadily expanding world-wide trade and new colonies in America and India. Ports and cities, especially London, grew in size and importance.

# LAW AND ORDER UNDER THE TUDORS

*KEY QUESTION*

◆ *How did the Tudor monarchs make England a more law-abiding country?*

In the last chapter we saw how the problem of the 'over-mighty subject' threatened law and order in England in the Middle Ages. In the 15th century this problem reached a peak, with the Wars of the Roses between rival groups of barons. Henry VII, founder of the Tudor line of monarchs, emerged victorious out of these wars in 1485. Henry did not have a good claim to the throne, but defeated his rivals and, with his successors, set about dealing with the problem of law and order.

## 1. Royal power and the over-mighty subject

● The law of **treason** was strengthened. It was made treasonable not just to rebel against the monarch, but to speak or write against him. The royal government was therefore controlling people's opinions, as well as their actions. Later, as we shall see, it tried to control their religious beliefs too. The punishment for treason was hanging, drawing and quartering, the most ferocious punishment in English law (see Punishment box).

*********\***PUNISHMENT BOX**********

The punishment for high treason was as follows, with an 18th-century explanation in quotation marks. They were first dragged through the streets, 'because they were not worthy any more to tread upon the earth', then hanged, 'by the neck between heaven and earth, because they were unworthy of both'. They were cut down while still alive and drawn (i.e. their entrails cut out and burnt in front of them) 'because they had inwardly conceived and harboured in their parts such horrible treason', then beheaded and quartered (i.e. cut into four pieces) 'because in their heads they had imagined such mischief'.

Purpose: to be a savage deterrent.

*******************************************

● Monarchs insisted that they were not just one of the barons, but were chosen by God to rule. To rebel was therefore a sin as well as a crime.

● Special royal law-courts were set up. The most famous was called **Star Chamber**. It began in 1487 and was just the king and his Council sitting as a court, in a room with painted stars on the ceiling. Star

## SOURCE 1

A woodcut showing the remains of John Stevens, hanged, drawn and quartered for treason in 1632.

## SOURCE 2

*The records of the city of Oxford list the expenses of the visit of the Assize judges:*

Accounts for 1583–1584.

For a gallon of wine given to the judges at the winter assizes 4s 4d [22p].

For 4 pairs of gloves given to them at the same time 13s 4d [67p].

Chamber was not bound by the ordinary legal procedures: there was no jury; it could torture suspects; punishments could be fierce, for example nose-slitting, ear-slicing, or branding.

● England's most lawless areas were on the borders, far from London and the monarch. The Council of the North was set up in York, to deal with law and order in the North. There was also a Council of the Welsh Marches.

● The main problem with over-mighty subjects was their gangs of followers (see page 31). In 1504 the Statute of Livery made it illegal to have large numbers of men wearing your livery (your badge). The Tudor monarchs made sure this was enforced. When the Earl of Oxford lined up 500 retainers, all wearing his livery, to bid farewell to Henry VIII, he was had up before Star Chamber and fined 15,000 marks (£10,000).

## 2. Local law and order

● Serious offences were dealt with by sending out **royal judges** to each county. They held the County Assizes twice a year, usually in the county town. It was a social occasion too, attended by all the important people in the county (see Source 2).

The session began with a ceremonial entry of the judges, followed by a sermon. The Grand Jury was then sworn in (see also page 21). The constable presented the offenders and the Grand Jury decided if there was a case to answer. If there was, a jury of 12 was sworn in from the offenders' local area. Trials were very short – rarely as much as an hour. Only about 20% of offences were crimes against the person and about 80% were crimes against property.

● **Justices of the Peace (JPs).** JPs had been set up in the Middle Ages (see page 21), but under the Tudors they became the key people in enforcing local law and order. They were unpaid and took on the job as a mark of their local importance (Source 3). Also, as well-off and established landowners, they had an interest in keeping law and order enforced. Tudor monarchs recognised this and were happy to use them, as their work did not cost the royal government anything. There were about 20 JPs per county.

### SOURCE 3

Portrait of a JP. JPs were drawn from the gentry class; that is, below the aristocracy but still substantial landowners.

### SOURCE 4

Two offenders in the pillory for selling underweight bread.

A JP, on his own, often in his own home, could decide some low-level offences such as drunkenness or fighting. Two or three JPs met regularly at a Petty Sessions for other offences and four times a year all the JPs in a county met to try all offences except those which had to wait for the Assize Judges. This was called the Quarter Sessions and here they were advised by someone with legal training. The Quarter Sessions was also an important local occasion, attended by up to 150 people. A Grand Jury, of perhaps 17, 19 or 21 (odd numbers so as to ensure a verdict) decided if there was a case to answer. If there was, a jury of 12 was sworn in. All the village and hundred constables had to attend. JPs could fine people, sentence them to the pillory, or the stocks (Sources 4 and 5) or to be whipped. At the Quarter Sessions they even had the power to sentence someone to death. In later Tudor times the Devon Quarter Sessions executed about four people a year.

However, in addition to their legal work, Tudor monarchs gave the JPs all sorts of other tasks. By the end of the reign of Queen Elizabeth, in 1603, they were responsible for enforcing 309 different laws. These covered such things as fixing wages and conditions of work, organising road-mending and bridge repair, licensing ale-houses, regulating local games like village football, checking weights and measures, and arresting vagrants (see page 42). In 1581 William Lambarde wrote a book to help JPs do their job; it was 600 pages long.

● **Constables.** There were other local law officials, of whom the most important was the village constable. In theory everyone in the village had to serve as a constable, but in fact most people paid someone to take their turn. This was a part-time job. Constables did not have a uniform nor any weapons, nor did they go out on patrol. They generally acted as the JPs' assistants, made arrests, and took convicts to jail.

SOURCE 5

A wandering musician in the stocks.

SOURCE 6

Woodcut picture of the bellman. In some towns the watchman was called the bellman. He carries a lantern, a bell, and a weapon, called a halberd.

## 3. Law and order in towns

Towns were still very small in Tudor England and only one person in ten lived in one. Apart from London, only Norwich and Bristol had over 10,000 people. However, with peaceful times and a rising population (see page 35) towns were growing.

● The Mayor and aldermen who ran towns were keen that their town should have a reputation for honesty and good business. They therefore, like the JPs in the countryside, enforced law and order. One of the best ways of punishing crooked trading was to display the criminal to the public in the pillory (Source 4). People could then know who they were and express their disapproval by throwing things at them. It was also the towns which suffered most from the problem of wandering vagabonds described on pages 42–43. Again, the stocks was a useful form of punishment (Source 5).

● The town equivalent of the village constable was the **watchman** or **bellman** (Source 6). He walked the streets at night, calling out the hours. His presence may have deterred thieves and probably comforted the townsfolk.

### \*\*\*\*\*\*\*\*\*\***PUNISHMENT BOX**\*\*\*\*\*\*\*\*\*\*
### Stocks and pillory

The purpose of these forms of punishment was public disgrace for the criminal. It was a 'shaming' punishment.

\*\*\*\*\*\*\*\*\*\*\*\*\*\*\*\*\*\*\*\*\*\*\*\*\*\*\*\*\*\*\*\*\*\*\*\*\*\*\*\*\*\*\*

SOURCE 7

*The account book of the town of Burford shows the expenses of buying some law enforcement equipment:*

1586. Was paid to Mr Alderman, Mr Chadwell and Richard Dalby for the making of the pillory and for a pair of stocks £4.10s 5d (£4.52p).

❖ *Were the Tudor monarchs dictators? (That is, could they do exactly as they liked, regardless of the law and popular opinion?)*
   *Think about:*
   *– Did they extend their power in new ways?*
   *– Were they cruel?*
   *– Were they fair?*
   *– Could they control local government?*
❖ *How did the monarchs control law and order at a local level?*
❖ *The system relied heavily on the JPs. What sort of people became JPs? In what ways was this a good idea and in what ways might it be unfair?*
❖ *How good was the Tudor system of law and order at dealing with:*
   *– a local drunk?*
   *– a gang of thieves?*
   *– a town pickpocket?*
   *– a highway robber mounted on horseback?*

# PROTEST: THE PILGRIMAGE OF GRACE, 1536 AND KETT'S REBELLION, 1549

## KEY QUESTION
◆ *Why did people rebel in Tudor times, even though rebellion was a serious crime and a sin?*

With no modern-style police or army to enforce obedience, Tudor monarchs put a lot of effort into ramming home to people the idea that rebellion was wrong. Bishops preached that rebellion was sinful (Source 1). Henry VIII's minister, Thomas Cromwell, paid writers to explain the dangers of upsetting the order of things in which some were born to rule and some were born to obey without questioning.

### SOURCE 1

Sermons about obedience:

(a) Bishop Latimer: 'If the king should require of you an unjust request, you are bound to pay it and not to resist or rebel . . . the king is wrong for asking an unjust thing, but God will reckon with him for it; you must not take it upon yourself to judge him.'

(b) Archbishop Whitgift: 'The rule of obedience that is between the ruler and his subject holds the same between the husband and the wife, the father and his child, the master and his servant.'

### SOURCE 2

Jervaulx Abbey. Monks from here joined the Pilgrimage of Grace.

Nevertheless, there were rebellions in Tudor England. We will look here at two rather different examples.

## The Pilgrimage of Grace, 1536

In 1536 England was in the middle of a religious upheaval. Henry VIII had declared himself the Head of the Church in England and broken away from Rome. He had divorced his wife, Catherine of Aragon. Thomas Cromwell had begun the dissolution of the monasteries.

The country was full of wild rumours about what the next change would be. In the North 55 monasteries and nunneries had been closed down. A popular protest began, mainly in Yorkshire. It had an able leader: Robert Aske, a lawyer from East Yorkshire with London connections. For most of the 30,000 'pilgrims', it was a religious protest. They took as their badge the banner of the five wounds of Christ (Source 3). Several monks joined them (Source 2). Aske also emphasised the religious element in his proclamations (Source 4).

The rebels occupied York on 15 October and restored a dissolved nunnery in the city. On 19 October, in a meeting at Pontefract, Aske pointed out the economic impact of the dissolution of the monasteries: in the sparsely populated North, monasteries played a big part in helping travellers and looking after the sick.

However, the five Articles Aske drew up show a wider range of complaints:

1. Restoration of dissolved monasteries and nunneries.
2. End to the Statute of Uses (changes in inheritance laws).
3. Reduction of taxes when people are in economic difficulty.
4. Thomas Cromwell (and Richard Rich) were bad advisers.
5. Some bishops were too Protestant in their beliefs.

Most important people in the North threw in their lot with the rebels. Aske's policy was to avoid bloodshed, sit tight, stay in the North, and overawe the government into giving way.

The government was forced to negotiate. The Duke of Norfolk met them to talk, but admitted to Henry: 'I beseech you to take in good part whatsoever promises I shall make to the rebels for surely I shall observe no part thereof.' An agreement was made to send two representatives to the king in London, with their petition, and a truce should be observed until they returned. The king played for time, but Aske held the rebellion together. In December the rebels were promised a Parliament to discuss all their grievances. They went home thinking they had won.

In 1537 Henry took his revenge. A failed armed rising in East Yorkshire gave him the excuse he needed to punish all the rebels. The Duke of Norfolk moved in to arrest the leaders. Aske was executed in York on 12 July and 178 others were also executed.

## SOURCE 3

The badge of the five wounds of Christ, an important medieval Roman Catholic symbol, worn by the rebels of the Pilgrimage of Grace.

## SOURCE 4

For this pilgrimage we have taken for the preservation of Christ's church, of this realm of England, the king our sovereign lord, the nobility and commons of the same, and with the intent of making petition to the king's highness for the reformation of that which is amiss within this his realm.

*Robert Aske's proclamation to York, October 1536.*

# Kett's Rebellion, 1549

1549 was also a crisis year. The 12-year-old Edward VI was king, while his uncle, the Duke of Somerset, ruled. A new and strongly Protestant prayer book had been introduced. There was serious inflation: some were doing well out of this, but others were suffering from high rents and high food prices. There was jealousy and resentment over enclosures – the fencing-off of common land by better-off landowners. They could then farm for profit in their own way, often keeping sheep, which employed far fewer people than arable farming. Somerset felt that these enclosures were causing serious poverty, unemployment and unrest. He set up a commission to investigate them and pardoned all those arrested for pulling down fences.

In this atmosphere, in July some people in Norfolk pulled down some fences across their common land. Two weeks later a larger gathering met to pull down the fences of a big landowner called Flowerdew. They found a leader in Robert Kett, who was himself a landowner and a rival of Flowerdew's. He led 16,000 people to Norwich and set up camp outside the city at Mousehold Heath. Four similar camps were set up elsewhere in Norfolk and Suffolk.

## The crisis in Norfolk

Social tension was bitter in Norfolk. The richest 6% of the population owned 60% of the land. This meant they were able to get richer while the poor got poorer. In particular, they used their right to graze huge flocks of sheep and cattle on the commons, then bought land and enclosed it. Thomas Townshend, for example, built up a flock of 4,000 sheep in the 1540s and his profits rose from £99 in 1545 to £133 in 1548. These actions had broken the trust between the governing class and the people on which local government depended.

These were the people which Kett and the rebels were protesting about. Indeed, they tried to make it clear they had no quarrel with Somerset and the king, whom they expected to agree with them.

11. We pray that tenants should take the profits of the commons and that lords should not use the commons.

21. We pray that it be not lawful for the lords of any manor to buy lands and let them out again, to their great profit and the undoing of your poor subjects.

29. We pray that no lord, knight, esquire, gentleman do graze or feed any bullocks or sheep but only for the provision of his house.

*Some extracts from the 29 demands of Kett's Rebels.*

A view of Norwich, with Mousehold Heath in the background. Robert Kett was hanged from the walls of Norwich Castle on 7 December 1549.

The rebels' list of 29 grievances was a very mixed bag. Some were purely local issues, like free navigation of the rivers. Some dealt with enclosures but some were to do with religion. The rebels were determinedly Protestant: they used the new Prayer Book in their services on Mousehold Heath. Their complaints were about ignorant priests, priests who dabbled in land dealings and priests who preferred to live in luxury in lords' mansions rather than attending to the people.

The rebels attacked and occupied Norwich at the end of July. In August a mercenary army was sent to Norfolk. On 24 August a battle was fought. 3,000 rebels were killed. The leaders were rounded up. Robert Kett was hanged from the walls of Norwich Castle on 7 December 1549.

❖ *Compare these two rebellions.*
*(i) Make a list of basic facts about each one: name, date, area where it took place, name of leader.*
*(ii) Compare aims. What was the main aim of the rebels? What other aims did they have?*
*What reasons do historians give for each rebellion? Are the historians' reasons the same as the aims that the rebels themselves put forward?*
*(iii) To rebel was a sin and a crime carrying the death penalty. How did the rebels try to avoid these dangers?*
*(iv) What tactics did the rebels use?*
❖ *Why did each rebellion fail?*
❖ *Write an essay of four paragraphs using points (i) to (iv) above.*
❖ *What do these two rebellions tell us about people in Tudor England?*

# POVERTY AND VAGRANCY

*KEY QUESTION*

◆ *Was it a crime to be poor?*

In every age there seems to be one kind of criminal whom everyone loves to hate. In the late 16th century it was the people they called 'vagabonds'. A vagabond was someone, usually a stranger, travelling around without a job or a home. After the upper-class law-breakers of the late Middle Ages, attention now turned to where blame was to rest for the next 400 years, the very poor. Respectable people looked at beggars or wandering tramps and were horrified. They made several assumptions about them (Source 2):

1. They were all criminals.
2. They belonged to organised criminal gangs who terrorised the countryside.
3. They were too lazy to find a job.
4. The problem was increasing.

Books were written about them (Source 3). These told a public, eager to be shocked, about an underworld of criminal vagabonds. They identified certain types: a **ruffler** carried a sword and pretended to be an ex-soldier looking for work but in fact was an armed robber; a **prigger of palfreys** was a horse-thief; a **hooker** stole things from open cottage windows by means of a long stick with a hook on the end; a **counterfeit crank** pretended to be disabled and begged, and so on.

**SOURCE 1**

A 17th-century drawing of beggars by the Dutch artist, Rembrandt. Do they look like a menace to society?

Savage laws were passed: by an Act of 1531 they could be whipped at a cart tail (Source 3). By an Act of 1547 they could be branded with a 'V' on the forehead. The thinking behind the Act of 1572, and the punishment it laid down, is shown in Source 2A.

**\*\*\*\*\*\*\*\*\*\*PUNISHMENT BOX\*\*\*\*\*\*\*\*\*\*\***

**Tudor vagrancy laws**

Punishment: mutilation or whipping

Purpose: To show society's disapproval; to make them change their ways; to deter others.

**\*\*\*\*\*\*\*\*\*\*\*\*\*\*\*\*\*\*\*\*\*\*\*\*\*\*\*\*\*\*\*\*\*\*\*\*\***

## Were vagabonds a threat to respectable society?

Let us look at the four assumptions made above. How true are they?

It is true that there were more unemployed people and beggars wandering about in the late 16th century.

It is true that the forces of law and order were very weak: only the JP and a part-time constable. When historians look at the records, however, assumptions 1, 2 and 3 do not seem to be true. Look at Source 4; how far does this evidence match the fears respectable people had? Even the last two, who were thieves, are hardly a gang of professional crooks.

**SOURCE 2**

**A** 'All parts of England and Wales be presently exceedingly pestered with rogues, vagabonds and sturdy beggars,\* who daily commit horrible murders, thefts and other outrages.' Anyone found guilty was to be tied to a cart and whipped, then branded through the gristle of the right ear with an inch-thick hot iron.

*\*A 'sturdy beggar' is someone who is able-bodied enough to work, but is living by begging.*

*From the beginning of the Act passed in 1572 to punish 'vagabonds'.*

**B** 'It was obvious to all men that beggars and thieves were everywhere. And we found the cause was that they were idle. And the cure must be to make them work.'

*Extract from the records of the Bridewell, London, 1553.*

## SOURCE 3

Vagabonds being 'whipped at a cart's tail', from the front cover of a book about vagabonds by Thomas Harman, published in 1567.

In fact, this was a time when the numbers of the very poor were increasing. Look at Source 5. What was happening to wages and prices? Did these changes make you better or worse off?

The rising population made this worse: there were too many people for the number of jobs available. Other Tudor changes also made the situation worse:

● Monasteries used to look after tramps and beggars. Henry VIII had closed them down.

● The Tudor monarchs had put an end to private armies ('retainers', see page 36).

● An increase in sheep-farming was throwing people out of work (see the story of Kett's rebellion, page 40).

● There was no dole. People with no job were forced to leave home to look for work.

Some people began to put forward an alternative to the policy of harsh punishment. Eventually the 1601 Poor Law was passed. This separated children, disabled and able-bodied poor. It allowed parishes to collect money – a poor rate – to deal with the poor. Many parishes set up a 'House of Correction' where the able-bodied poor were put to work. Every parish had to look after its own poor and poor people had to stay in their home parish, and not wander about. This system lasted until 1834. It worked quite well in many cases, depending on the attitude of the overseers who ran it.

## SOURCE 4

Girl from Cheltenham, going to look for work in the north.

Richard Boney 'He has worked for several men but confesses that many times he has made a living begging.'

Two vagabonds from the north confessed to stealing ducks, geese and pigs on their travels, which they either ate there and then or sold to buy somewhere to stay.

*Extracts from the town records of Warwick in the reign of Elizabeth concerning vagabonds.*

## SOURCE 5

*Population, wages and prices in the 16th century.*

Population of England: 1520 – about 2.25 million;
1603 – about 3.75 million.

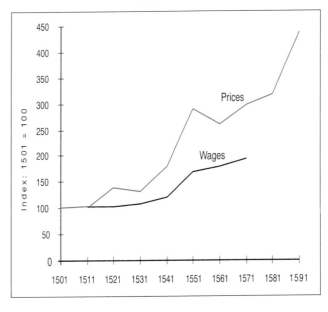

❖ *Write an analysis of the law and the poor in Elizabethan England. Here are your paragraph openings:*
*1. 'In Elizabethan England many people thought that vagabonds were . . .' (Quote important sentences from Source 2 to support your points).*
*2. 'They were a real threat to society because . . .' (Look back at page 37)*
*3. 'Historians think that they were not really a threat to society because . . .' (Look at Source 4)*
*4. 'The real reasons for the increase in the number of wandering poor people were . . .' (Look at Source 5)*
*5. 'The purpose of the anti-vagabond laws of the 16th century was . . .'*
*6. 'They were successful/unsuccessful because . . .'*

# PROTEST: HERESY AND THE GUNPOWDER PLOT

## KEY QUESTION
◆ *Who were heretics and how were they treated?*

Governments make the laws. In the 16th and 17th centuries the laws included controlling your religious beliefs. If you did not have the same religious belief as the government you were called a **heretic** and could be punished, even put to death.

In the early 16th century everyone in England belonged to the Roman Catholic Church, as they had done for centuries. We saw on page 36 that Henry VIII broke with the Roman Catholic Church. Those who refused to accept this break were executed, including his former friend and minister, Sir Thomas More. Henry's son Edward (1547–1553), continued the break with Rome but he was succeeded by Henry's elder daughter, Mary.

## Heretics under Queen Mary (1553–1558)

Mary was determined to restore Roman Catholicism to England. One of her ways of doing this was to execute those she regarded as heretics. The usual way of executing heretics was by burning them. Source 1 shows the execution by burning of Latimer and Ridley, both of whom had been bishops in the reign of Henry VIII. However, most of the 280 or so men and women burnt in Mary's reign were ordinary people. They believed so strongly in their Protestant faith that they would rather die than change it.

Death by burning was a long and horrible business, taking about an hour. Often relatives would try to hasten the end by hanging a bag of gunpowder round the victim's neck, or rushing into the flames and ending it all with a knife.

## SOURCE 1

The burning of Latimer and Ridley, as Protestant heretics, in 1555.

## Heretics under Queen Elizabeth (1558–1603)

Elizabeth brought England back to Protestantism. As the reign went on, England became involved in war with Catholic Spain. The Pope said that Elizabeth was not the rightful ruler, so Catholics could rebel against her. There were also plots to kill her and replace her with a Roman Catholic monarch. Her advisers believed that Roman Catholics were a danger to her government. They were fined for not going to church. Many were arrested and tried, not for heresy, but for treason. Altogether about 250 Roman Catholics were executed in Elizabeth's reign as traitors. The punishment for treason was death by hanging, drawing and quartering (see page 36), not burning.

How did ordinary people react to these changing laws about what they were supposed to believe? Obviously most people went along to church every Sunday and kept their views to themselves. Obviously, quite a number didn't, and died for their beliefs. A few decided that Elizabeth was not God's choice as ruler and tried to overthrow her government.

# *ACTIVITY*

✧ *Amnesty International monitors the actions of governments today. They frequently report cases of governments torturing or putting to death their opponents. They calculate that over half of all the governments in the world use torture.*

✧ *Contact Amnesty International for their Schools Pack. Where in the world today is torture being used? Who are its victims?*

## *********PUNISHMENT BOX***********

### Heresy laws

Heretics, in England and elsewhere, were burnt at the stake.

Purpose: To utterly destroy someone who the government regarded as a wicked person.

***************************************

## The Gunpowder Plot

To a government, trying to overthrow it is the worst of all crimes: treason. Throughout history therefore the worst tortures and the most horrific punishments have been reserved for those who try to overthrow the government. All governments also use secret methods to find out what their enemies are plotting.

The Gunpowder Plot of 1605 is an interesting example of these measures being taken by an English government in the early 17th century.

## What was the aim of the Gunpowder Plot?

The motive for the plotters was religion: they were Roman Catholics. Elizabeth was succeeded in 1603 by King James VI of Scotland, who became King James I of England. At first he stopped the heavy fines Roman Catholics had to pay for non-attendance at Church. Then the fines began again and a group of Roman Catholics decided to assassinate the king. In the box below, the left-hand side tells the story of the plot as explained by the king's chief minister, Robert Cecil. In recent years, however, historians have found some problems with Cecil's version. These are given on the right-hand side.

### CECIL'S VERSION

The plotters decided to blow up James at the state opening of Parliament. They began to dig a tunnel under the House of Lords, but met a thick wall. They then rented a cellar right under the House of Lords. They filled this with 36 barrels of gunpowder. Just before the state opening, one of the plotters, Francis Tresham, wrote an anonymous letter to his brother-in-law, Lord Mounteagle, warning him. Mounteagle showed the letter to Cecil and James, who decided to search the cellars on the evening of 5 November 1605. One of the plotters, Guy Fawkes, was found, with the gunpowder. He was tortured for four days (see Sources 3, 4 and 5) and revealed the plot. The plotters were tracked down. Four were shot and the rest brought to London. They were found guilty of treason and put to death in January 1606.

### Problems

1. No one saw any of the earth dug out of the first tunnel, nor was it ever found.

2. They rented the cellar from a friend of Robert Cecil's; this friend died on 5 November.

3. All gunpowder was owned by the government and kept in the Tower of London; how did the plotters get hold of so much?

4. The letter to Lord Mounteagle looks as if it might be forged.

5. Francis Tresham was not arrested with the others. Once they had been tried he was arrested and died mysteriously in the Tower two weeks later.

### SOURCE 2

My Lord, have a care for your safety. I would advise you to devise some excuse to miss your attendance at this Parliament. Go into the country, for they shall receive a terrible blow this Parliament – and yet they shall not see who hurts them.

*Letter from one of the plotters, Francis Tresham, to his brother-in-law, Lord Mounteagle.*

### SOURCE 3

If he will not otherwise confess, the gentler tortures are to be used first, and then the uttermost pain.

*King James instructs the use of torture on Guy Fawkes.*

❖ *In pairs, think about the five problems in the box above. What do you think is the explanation for each?*
❖ *Do you think Cecil knew about the plot before 5 November? What is your evidence for this?*
❖ *What are the weaknesses in Cecil's account?*
❖ *What do you think is the REAL story of the Gunpowder Plot?*

### SOURCE 4

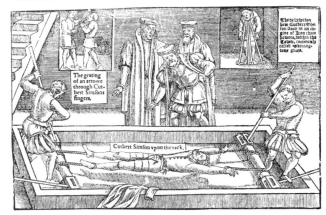

The rack, the torture instrument probably used on Guy Fawkes. The victim's body was gradually stretched.

### SOURCE 5
Guy Fawkes' signature before (above) and after (below) he was tortured.

# THE WITCHCRAFT CRAZE

## KEY QUESTION

◆ *Why was there a witchcraft craze in the 16th and 17th centuries?*

From about the middle of the 16th century to about the end of the 17th, 3,000 people were tried for witchcraft in England, 90% of them women, most of them over 50 years old. 400 were hanged and many more died in prison. Some were killed by villagers, because it was believed that if you shed a witch's blood her curse would end. In the county of Essex 317 women and 23 men were tried for witchcraft between 1560 and 1680. Over 100 were hanged. There were two peaks of witchcraft trials – the 1560s and the 1640s; in one year, 1645, there were 36 witch trials in Essex.

Why was there this extraordinary witch craze? After all, this period was not the first time in history that there were strange old women living on their own, or village quarrels.

## Government interest

As we have already seen, this was a time of great strife. Governments were insecure, facing rebellions, plots, invasion and civil war. As we also saw (on page 36), governments expected to control people's beliefs and to punish those with views they did not approve of. Many educated people really believed in astrology, charms and spells. King James VI of Scotland (King James I of England) certainly believed in witches and wrote a book about them (Source 1). Many books were published, describing what witches did. Some people set out to find witches. The most notorious was Matthew Hopkins, who called himself 'Witchfinder-General' and brought dozens of witches to trial in East Anglia during the 1640s.

The first law against witchcraft was in 1542. An Act of 1563 brought the death penalty for 'invoking evil spirits and using witchcraft, charms or sorcery whereby any person shall happen to be killed or destroyed.' There was another Act in 1604.

## SOURCE 1

There are so many at this time and in this country of these detestable slaves of the devil, the witches, that it has encouraged me to write this book so I can convince the doubting hearts of many, that such assaults by Satan are practised.

*King James explains why he wrote a book on witchcraft in 1597.*

## Village tensions

These were difficult times for ordinary people too. There were several causes of tension:

● **Religious.** After so many rapid changes they were uncertain about what to believe.

● **Political.** There were the arguments which led to the Civil War.

● **Economic**. Prices were rising faster than wages (see page 43). Many villagers were living on the edge of existence and a bad harvest could mean starvation. So could an accident, which prevented you from working, or a sudden illness to your animals.

● **Social.** Some villagers were doing well and becoming better off; some were not. The differences were greater than in the Middle Ages. Those who suffered most were single elderly women.

It is perhaps not surprising that the peak years for witchcraft trials were during the religious uncertainties of the 1560s and in the middle of the Civil War in the 1640s.

## SOURCE 2

Some woman falls out with her neighbour. There follows some minor disaster. A suspicion arises. Within a few years she is in some jar with another. He is also afflicted. The village gossips far and wide: Mother W is a witch, she has bewitched Mr B and two hogs have died unexpectedly. Her neighbours dare not say anything but in their hearts they wish she was hanged.

Shortly afterwards someone else falls sick. He doesn't eat and can't sleep. The neighbours come to visit him. 'Well, neighbour', says one, 'Did you ever anger Mother W?' 'Truly neighbour' says he, 'I cannot tell how I have displeased her, unless it was the other day, when my wife asked her to keep her hens out of my garden.'

Everybody now says that Mother W is a witch. It is beyond all doubt, because someone saw a weasel run from her yard into his just before he was taken ill. The sick man dies, believing he is bewitched. Then Mother W is arrested and sent to prison.

*George Gifford, writing in 1587, describes how an accusation of witchcraft could build up.*

When we look at court records we find that the activities of outside investigators like Matthew Hopkins are rare. Much more common is the slow build-up of tension in the village described by George Gifford in Source 2. His is an imaginary account, but written at the time. We can see how a village quarrel could break out. The accusation of witchcraft provided the explanation for the small, but, to a poor family, serious disasters, such as an accident or sudden illness.

## Witch trials

The accusation of witchcraft was so serious because trials were so unreliable. How do you prove someone is in league with the Devil?

● The accused could be 'floated' (Source 3). The water was blessed by a priest and the accused thrown in with their hands tied in front of them in the shape of the cross. If they floated they were guilty, as the holy water was rejecting them. If they sank they were innocent, and could be hauled out, but judges often left them some time to be sure. The experience would be enough to kill an old person.

● The accused's body could be searched for unusual marks, supposedly left by the devil's assistants when they sucked the witch's blood.

● The accused might 'confess'. Often they were kept awake for days and nights on end. Modern torturers find this is an extremely effective way of obtaining confessions. After a few days of 'sleep deprivation' the accused will agree to anything (Source 4).

● Two other 'proven' witches could swear that the accused was a witch.

## The end of witchcraft

By the end of the 17th century attitudes were changing. People no longer believed in all the strange mumbo-jumbo of witchcraft. The last hanging was in 1682; the last witchcraft trial was in 1712 and witchcraft ceased to be an offence in 1736.

A case in Tring, Hertfordshire, shows how things had changed by 1751. Some villagers had arranged a 'floating' of Ruth Osborne, whom they suspected of witchcraft. She died, and Thomas Colley, a local chimney-sweep who had taken part in the accusation, was tried and executed for her murder.

### ******PUNISHMENT BOX******

#### Witchcraft laws

Witches could be hanged if they caused someone's death or on a second offence.

Purpose: To destroy a wicked person; to deter others.

**************************

**SOURCE 3**

A 16th-century print showing a woman being tried for witchcraft by being 'floated'.

**SOURCE 4**

Then said the judge: 'Agnes Waterhouse, when did your cat suck your blood?' 'Never' said she. 'No', said he, 'Let me see'. And then the gaoler lifted her kerchief from her head and there were various spots on her face and one on her nose. Then said the judge 'In good faith, Agnes, when did he suck of thy blood last?' 'By my faith, good lord' said she 'not for a fortnight'.

*Agnes Waterhouse confesses to being a witch, Essex, 1569. She was executed, the first of the Essex witches to die.*

❖ *Why did witchcraft become a criminal offence in the 16th century?*
❖ *Which was the more important cause of the witch craze: the government; individual leaders; the general public? Explain your answer.*
❖ *Why did villagers accuse people of witchcraft?*
❖ *What does the witch craze tell us about the position of women and attitudes towards women in 17th-century Britain?*
❖ *How have historians' researches into Court records helped our understanding of the witch craze?*
❖ *Why did the witch craze die out?*

# WOMEN AND THE LAW

## KEY QUESTIONS

◆ *How did the law affect women in early modern times?*
◆ *How had this changed from medieval times?*
◆ *How were women involved in 'social crime'?*

Legally, women were still as subject to men as they had been in medieval times (see page 26 and Source 1). In law, a woman still had to obey her father or husband; she could not choose her husband and if he chose to squander her money after marriage she could not stop him; she could not trade or own property; she could not divorce him, or gain custody of the children if he divorced her. The universities, the Church, Parliament and medicine were still all closed to her. She could not be a JP. She still had to behave in ways men found acceptable – the ducking stool (see Source 2 on page 26) was in use until 1819.

## Changing customs

### Businesswomen

In theory, women needed their husband's permission to take part in trade or business, and records (there are many more records for this period than for medieval times), show that by the 16th century this was more common. Women were often market-traders and shopkeepers. Widows were usually allowed to take over their dead husband's business and some women traded in their own right. For example, Widow Phillips ran a carrier's business and received £1.4/- (£1.20p) for carrying armour for 260 men and 20 barrels of bullets for the Parliamentary army in the Civil War; Lady Margaret Crumpe invested in the slave-ship 'Dorothy' in 1707. Wills, like the one in Source 2, show that, while not rich, some women were not badly off.

Other evidence, however, contradicts this. It shows that women were still second-class members of the business community: very few women were allowed to take on apprentices (only 2% of London apprentices in the 16th century). Women were also the first to be excluded from guilds in hard times: the guild merchants in Preston had 16 women members in 1397, 6 in 1415, 1 in 1542 and none after that. Only in the 18th century did the hold of guilds on trade loosen, to women's advantage.

### Freedom

Of course, the legal status of women did not always reflect the real position. The Dutchman, van Meteren, commented on the freedom exercised by Englishwomen in daily life. They were free to go to market, visit friends, or sit outside their front doors chatting. Some independence had always been available to rich women, but this increased in the 17th century, as Source 3 shows.

### Strict settlement

The law of land inheritance changed during the 17th century. Strict settlement became more common. This meant that all the heirs of an estate, including the widow, received an income from it. This might be less than the third previously allowed as a 'dower' to the widow (see page 27).

### Women and crime

● **The double standard.** Women often received harsher punishment for the same offence. For example, Thomas Mace and his wife were both found guilty of being drunk in Norwich one Sunday in 1633, but only his wife was put in the stocks. The number of women tried for fighting each other might reflect male disgust at behaviour which would be ignored if two men were involved.

### SOURCE 1

After marriage, all the will of the wife, in judgement of the law, is subject to the will of the husband. She is a 'feme coverte'.

*A handbook on the law for JPs, published in 1653. 'Feme coverte' was the legal term for a married woman, under the protection of her husband.*

### SOURCE 2

I give to my daughters, Margaret and Martha, my chest of linen, to be equally divided between them. I give to Margaret the bedstead in my chamber next to the hall. Also to her the lesser of my two brass pots and two brass candlesticks. I give to Martha Feldgate [a grandchild] the bed in the parlour, with bedding. I give to my daughter Margaret six pieces of my best pewter, the biggest brass kettle but one and the chest in my parlour. I give to my daughter Martha the cupboard and table in the parlour. I give to the poor of Combs 40/- [£2].

*The will of Martha Barton, a widow, who died at Combs, Suffolk in 1630.*

- **Female criminals.** Female crime accounted for about 20% of all indictments. The figure for 20th-century Britain is nearer 10%. This does not mean that there were more women criminals, just that certain acts, such as adultery and bastardy, were crimes then but not now. Most female theft was small-scale: pickpocketing and shoplifting. Women were more likely to appear in the courts in years of high food prices, suggesting that they were driven to crime by hardship. The notorious 'Mal Cutpurse' (Source 4) was highly exceptional.

- **Women in court.** Women appeared in Church courts to protect their status or reputation. For example, in 1584 two women fought in St Ebbe's church, Oxford, over who should have the best pew; many of the cases of defamation tried in Durham were brought by women who felt their character had been damaged. However, women were more likely to appear in court as victims than as the accused. In East Sussex in the 17th century women were victims in 17% of all robberies and 50% of all murders. The law of 'feme coverte' meant that married woman could not bring a prosecution in court and all lawyers, magistrates, judges, jurors, constables and sheriffs were men: the law was a man's world, in which the evidence of a female witness was worth less than a male witness.

SOURCE 4

Mary Frith (aka Mal Cutpurse) 1589–1663, famous London gang-leader and cross-dresser. She is said to have robbed General Fairfax of £200.

## Women rioters

There were plenty of violent protest riots in the 17th and 18th centuries but they were quite different from those of the 19th. Many were about food prices and had quite limited aims: the rioters had no intention of overthrowing their rulers, but felt that the upper classes should behave reasonably. The historian E. P. Thompson has called this 'the moral economy of the crowd'.

Many such riots were led by women. After all, women shoppers were the first to find out about rising prices of food. They may also have believed that as married women had no rights at law, they could not be held responsible. In 1608 a grain ship in Southampton was boarded and unloaded by a group of women; in Oxford in 1693 poor women rioted at high corn prices and pelted millers and bakers with stones.

Women also objected to enclosures: in Giggleswick, Yorkshire, in 1533, 400 people, mainly women and children, rioted against the Earl of Cumberland's enclosure of common land. In 1659, in Dunchurch, Warwickshire, 15 women dug up fences and hedges by night. In this case, their husbands and fathers were prosecuted along with the women, even though they had acted on their own. The law's view was their menfolk were responsible for all their actions.

SOURCE 3

Portrait of the Countess of Arundel in 1618. She was the grand-daughter of Bess of Hardwick, and a rich woman. The portrait shows her in the London house she helped to design.

# 'GOING WEST': PUBLIC HANGING AND THE BLOODY CODE

## KEY QUESTIONS

◆ *What was the Bloody Code and what was its purpose?*

◆ *Did it lead to more people being hanged?*

## The triumph of the 'men of property'

The real winners after all the Civil Wars and conflicts of the 17th century in England were the 'men of property': mainly those who owned landed estates, with a few bankers and merchants. Royal power was weakened for ever: Star Chamber and other special royal courts were abolished by Parliament in 1641. The power to arrest someone without charge was blocked by the Habeas Corpus Act of 1679. These men of property had run their local areas as JPs since the 16th century; now they controlled Parliament as well. Yet they still had no police force or army to keep order over a growing population, probably 6.5 million by 1750.

## What kinds of laws did they pass?

They believed that, in the words of John Locke: 'Government has no end but the preservation of property.' Most of the laws were therefore designed to do just that. A good example is the Game Laws against poaching (for more on poaching see page 114).

At the same time, they greatly increased the number of offences for which you could be hanged. 'Capital offences', as they were called, increased from about 50 to over 200 from 1688 to 1820. This included stealing goods of a value over 5/- (25p) from a shop, stealing a sheep, pilfering from the docks, rioting against high food prices or stealing from a shipwreck.

This was the most ferocious legal system in Europe and was called (later) the Bloody Code. The death penalty was customarily added to Acts of Parliament which were really dealing with something else; for example, you could be hanged for damaging Westminster Bridge, or impersonating a Chelsea Pensioner.

**SOURCE 1**
An 18th-century judge.

**SOURCE 2**

With a face of solemn sorrow, adjusting the cap of judgement [a black square cap] on his head, His Lordship takes this golden opportunity to do good. He addresses the consciences of the trembling criminals . . . shows them how just and necessary it is that there should be laws to remove out of society those who, instead of contributing their honest labour to the public good, have exerted every wit that the blackest villainy can suggest. He tells them that death will be certain and speedy . . . and on this theme he may so speak as to melt, not only the wretches at the bar into feeling sorry for themselves, but the whole audience into deepest concern. Many of the most thoughtless among them may, for the rest of their lives, be saved from taking the first steps towards crime, which they now see will lead them towards destruction. The dreadful sentence is now pronounced, every heart shakes with terror and the almost fainting criminals are taken from the court.

*A judge passes the death sentence, 1785.*

**SOURCE 4**

The condemned man approaches the gallows at Tyburn.

## Public hangings

The whole purpose of the Bloody Code was to frighten people into being law-abiding citizens. At the Assize Court, the judge would give a little lecture, supposedly to the condemned man, but really to the packed public gallery (see Sources 1 and 2). It was widely believed that one little sin led straight to serious crime and the gallows. The 'confessions', extracted from the condemned by the Ordinary of Newgate (Source 3), always told the same story. Hogarth's picture of a public hanging (Source 4), is actually the last in a series called 'The Idle Apprentice' in which a young apprentice starts by playing dice instead of going to church and ends on the gallows.

Public hangings in the 18th century were extraordinary affairs, especially in London. Hangings were carried out at Tyburn in west London (hence the expression 'gone west'), where Marble Arch now stands. The condemned man would try to 'make a good end'. He would get a good suit of clothes. The three-mile trip from Newgate gaol might take two hours as he was allowed to stop at pubs on the way.

Source 4 shows the end of the journey. The condemned man is accompanied in the cart by his coffin and a priest. A huge crowd has come to watch, complete with orange-sellers and pickpockets. A temporary grandstand has been put up for spectators. His 'true confession' is being sold by the woman facing us. The Ordinary of Newgate is in his coach. The Tyburn gallows had three-posts – it was called 'the triple tree' and could hang up to nine people at a time. The hangman can be seen, smoking his pipe, on the top, adjusting the rope. This was tied round the condemned man's neck and the cart then driven away. It could take up to half an hour to die (in fact, one or two survived), but sometimes relatives would pull on the dying man's legs to finish him off.

Even that wasn't the end of it. London hospitals needed bodies for student doctors to dissect. They paid people to seize bodies from the gallows, but the crowd often objected to this. They apparently thought that while hanging was alright, dissection wasn't. Riots would break out. This explains the presence of the soldiers in Source 4.

**\*\*\*\*\*\*\*\*\*\*\*PUNISHMENT BOX\*\*\*\*\*\*\*\*\*\***

**Public hangings**

The purpose of public hangings was to deter others.

**\*\*\*\*\*\*\*\*\*\*\*\*\*\*\*\*\*\*\*\*\*\*\*\*\*\*\*\*\*\*\*\*\*\*\*\*\*\***

❖ *Read Source 5.*
❖ *What happened to the numbers of people hanged over the period from the late 16th to the early 18th centuries?*
❖ *How do items (a) and (b) help to explain the trend shown in item (c)?*
❖ *What do these figures tell us about: 18th-century judges? 18th-century juries?*

### SOURCE 3

I will get you as handsome a coffin as ever anyone ever set his arse in if you will only give me a few pages of confession.

*A condemned man is put under pressure to write a confession by the 'Ordinary' (the chaplain) at Newgate Prison.*

### SOURCE 5

The courts and the death sentence.

(a) In Elizabethan Essex 26% of accused people on capital charges (those carrying the death penalty) received a death sentence. In the early 18th century only 10% did.

(b) In Surrey in the late 16th century 54% of those sentenced to death were actually hanged. In the early 18th century only 35% were.

(c) Number of hangings per year in Cheshire:
    1580–89 – about 9 a year
    1620–29 – about 17 a year
    1700–09 – about 1 a year

In fact, courts tried not to use the death penalty. For example, the sum stolen was often falsely brought down below the hanging level, even to the ridiculous extent of listing the item stolen as 'Five pounds, value 10d'. Judges preferred to sentence people to transportation (see page 68). Witnesses would swear to the 'good character' of the accused, so as to reduce the sentence.

The result was that, despite the Bloody Code, fewer people were actually hanged. The attitude among the ruling classes seems to have been that capital punishment was there to frighten the masses into obedience, and so must regularly be used. However, it must not be used so often that the people would be disgusted and rise up against their rulers. It suited the powerful to be seen to be merciful on occasion. The down side was that whether you were hanged or not was largely a matter of luck: whether you had powerful friends, or if the judge liked your face.

# JONATHAN WILD AND 18TH-CENTURY CRIME

## KEY QUESTION
◆ *What class did most criminals belong to?*

This question may seem crazy to us: in our own time if someone from the upper classes comes before the courts it is news in itself. However, in Chapter 2 we saw that in the Middle Ages the upper classes were frequently in trouble with the law. To some extent this continued in the Early Modern period. People were hot-tempered, and usually carried weapons. In 1662 Charles Sackville, Earl of Dorset, was accused of murdering someone during a drunken night out. In 1681 the Earl of Eglinton killed a Mr Maddox after a quarrel between the two of them over a game of cards in an alehouse in Doncaster. Publicists for the government made much of the execution, in 1760, of Lord Ferrers, for murder: they used it to show how impartial the law was. In fact, these cases were extremely rare: most criminals in this period were from the lower classes.

◆ *Was there organised crime in the 18th century?*

## Rural crime

Smuggling was a major activity in the 18th century, as you will see on page 54. In some areas poaching was well-planned (see page 114). Horse-stealing seems to have been as organised as car theft nowadays; that is, sometimes it was, but in some cases it was just someone acting on impulse. Apart from these examples, most rural crime was almost all low level, petty and individual. However, there is a lack of evidence: maybe there were organised gangs, or families, of criminals in some villages or provincial towns, as there are today.

## London crime

London in the mid-18th century was the largest city in Europe, with over 500,000 people. It was also a port, a commercial centre, a huge market, an entertainment centre and a gathering place: the opportunities for crime were therefore enormous. However, was the crime organised? That is, was the pickpocket in Source 2 doing it for himself, or was he part of a gang?

Many people had long believed London crime was organised. Back in Elizabeth's reign, her minister Lord Burghley had been told of a child pickpockets' den, (Source 1). This seems similar to Fagin's den, as described by Dickens 250 years later in *Oliver Twist*.

## SOURCE 1

'One Wotton, a gentleman born, has a schoolhouse set up to teach young boys how to cut purses.' There was a teaching aid: a purse hung with bells. 'He that could take a piece of silver out of the purse without the noise of any of the bells was adjudged a LITTLE NIPPER.'

*Extract from a report sent to Lord Burghley in 1585.*

## SOURCE 2

A pickpocket at work.

Prostitution was probably organised (Source 3). However, the extraordinary story of Jonathan Wild certainly shows how one man came to be the Al Capone of his day.

## SOURCE 3

In 1608 Margaret Ferneseed published her story before being burnt at the stake for murdering her husband. (At that time, husband-murder was defined as 'petty treason' – because a husband was the little monarch in the family – so carried this severe sentence.) She proclaimed her innocence of the murder, but admitted to running a prostitution business. She watched the wagons arriving in London from the provinces so that she could 'make spoil of young maidens who were sent out of the country by their friends, here with hope to advance themselves'. They had to give 'ten shillings (50p) a week to her out of their gettings'. She also persuaded discontented wives to take part, and then forced them to continue by blackmailing them that she would tell their husbands.

## Jonathan Wild

Jonathan Wild was born in 1682 in Wolverhampton. He learnt the typical local trade of buckle-maker, got married and had a son. Then things went wrong and in 1706 he tried his luck in London. However, he was soon in debt and was put in a debtors' prison.

Here, as so often happens, his criminal career began. He met up with other crooks and decided to go into business as a receiver of stolen property. He then had a brilliant idea: after a theft he would go to the person who had been robbed and offer to give back the goods in return for a reward as long as the thief was not prosecuted. He soon found that victims of crime offered more money than the goods were worth to him as stolen property. If the thief objected, Wild would turn him in to the law.

He was tremendously successful. He wiped out gangs he did not control by informing on them. He said he was doing a service to the public by handing over thieves, and claimed to have sent over 200 to the gallows. He would walk in front of the cart to Tyburn (see page 50) calling out 'Here come my children!' He liked to use the title of 'Thieftaker-General' (Source 4). Soon he controlled most of the theft in London. He claimed to have organised this by dividing up the city and the main roads out of it into territories, one for each of his gangs.

He no longer visited victims of theft himself, but set up a 'lost property office', with lists of stolen goods he held in secret warehouses. In 1722 he bought a ship to send stolen goods to be sold abroad. It was also used to smuggle brandy, lace, silk and tea on the return trip. He employed teams of craftsmen to melt down silver and gold, and to re-set precious gems in new jewellery.

He travelled around in a coach pulled by six horses and was even asked by the government to suggest ways of controlling highwaymen. (He advised putting up the reward money.) Crooks, lawyers and victims crowded to see him in his rooms, where he breakfasted each day on a pint of sherry and a bowl of hot chocolate.

Eventually he lost the sympathy of the public by betraying a popular thief and escape expert, Jack Sheppard. A new law was passed in 1719 to catch him, making it a crime to take a reward for returning stolen goods without passing on information about the thief. He was arrested and found guilty. He appealed to the king on the grounds that he had turned in so many criminals, but was executed in 1725 (Source 4).

SOURCE 4

Jonathan Wild, Thieftaker-General. This poster is a joke invitation to his hanging in 1725.

A good deal of the story above is based on Wild's own claims, but even the basics of his career are pretty spectacular. There appear to have been, even before he got involved, gangs of thieves and organised receivers of stolen property.

However, the court records mostly tell a different tale. They are full of drunks, sellers of bad fish, runaway apprentices, cheats, vagrants and amateur prostitutes. The thieving is all small-scale and done on the spur of the moment. The motive is survival, not running a criminal business. These hundreds of modest law-breakers are nearer the reality of London crime than Jonathan Wild.

❖ *Jonathan Wild was tremendously popular for a while in the 1720s. Why do people admire some criminals, but not others?*

# SMUGGLING

### KEY QUESTION
◆ *Why was smuggling such big business?*

Smuggling in mid-18th century England is an excellent example of a crime created by the government. Smugglers are people who bring goods into (or take goods out of) a country without paying **customs duty** (tax) on them. In the 1700s most of the government's **revenue** (the money they needed to run the country) came from customs duties paid on goods imported or exported. Government policy was to protect British industry by putting high duties on foreign-made goods. Goods which could be smuggled into the country without paying customs duties were therefore cheaper than goods which had been legally imported. In the 17th century tobacco was smuggled into the country, mainly through Devon and Cornwall. The government also put duties on the export of goods which British industry needed, like wool. For a while wool-smugglers, called 'owlers', flourished in Sussex.

In the 1720s and 1730s high duties – 30% or more of the price – were put on some foreign imports. These gave smugglers their opportunity. The ideal goods to smuggle were things which lots of people wanted, expensive and not too bulky: brandy, tea and silk were favourites.

All that was needed was a little money and organisation. A 'venturer' put up the money to buy the goods in France or Holland. You needed a reliable captain of a fast ship, able to carry a good-sized cargo across the Channel in about eight hours. A 'lander' would arrange for small boats to meet the ship about three miles out at sea, usually at night, and bring the 'contraband' ashore on some remote beach (Source 1). It was then hidden until it could be taken up to London, or another large town, and sold. This was also usually done in the small hours of the night, and the wagonloads of smuggled goods would be gone from the town before daybreak.

Smuggling increased enormously as it was very

### SOURCE 1

A gang of smugglers landing barrels.

profitable. The government estimated that by 1784, 3 million pounds of tea were being smuggled into Britain each year, compared with 1 million pounds legally imported. Many ordinary people in the counties of south-east England – especially Sussex, Kent and Hampshire – were involved. The smugglers worked in gangs, sometimes 50 or 100 strong (Source 2). Some gangs dealt with 20 or 30 cargoes a week. You could earn 10/6 (52.5p) for a night's work, carrying two 4.5 gallon tubs of brandy up from the beach to its hiding-place. This was more than farm labourers earned in a week. A horse was provided and you also got a share of the profits. The pay was 12/7 (63p) for a night's work on one of the boats which landed the contraband. Other people, often quite respectable citizens, lent their barns or cellars as hiding-places.

### SOURCE 2

The smugglers pass and re-pass, to and from the seaside, 40 and 50 in a gang, in the daytime, loaded with tea and brandy. Above 200 mounted smugglers were seen one night upon the sea-beach there [Lydd, in Kent], waiting for the loading of six boats. They went in a body from the beach about four miles into the country and then separated into small parties.

*A Report to the Excise Commissioners, 1734.*

## SOURCE 3

Contemporary engraving of smugglers breaking open the Custom House at Poole, Dorset.

## SOURCE 4

The smugglers reigned a long time uncontrolled . . . If any of them happened to be taken, and the proof ever so clear against him, no magistrate in the county durst commit him to gaol. If he did he was sure to have his house or his barns set on fire, if he was so lucky to escape with his life.

*Report to the Duke of Richmond, 1749.*

## Violence and threats

Smuggling, like highway robbery (see page 56), has a romantic image. In fact the smugglers were often ruthless and used violence to avoid capture. They waged what was virtually a civil war against the government's Customs Officers. In 1736 the death penalty was brought in for wounding a Customs Officer.

One famous incident in 1746 involved the notorious gang based on the village of Hawkhurst, in Kent. One night the Customs Officers seized 2 tons of tea and 39 barrels of rum and brandy from its hiding-place. The Hawkhurst Gang armed themselves and followed the Customs Officers to Poole, in Dorset, where they broke open the Customs House and took back their goods (Source 3). Crowds of people cheered them home to Kent. However, one of the smugglers tossed a bag of tea to his friend, Chater, as he was going home. When the smuggler was arrested the authorities called in Chater for questioning. But before he could be questioned, he, and the Customs Officer with him, were brutally murdered.

## SOURCE 5

*One smuggler, hanged in 1749, told a priest:*

As to the charge of smuggling, he owned he had been engaged in that trade for a great many years, and did not think there was any harm in it.

As you saw in Chapter 2, those prepared to use violence can make the law impossible to operate. As Source 4 explains, magistrates were often afraid to convict smugglers. Informers were attacked in the street. Popular feeling was that 'Informers ought to be hanged. It is no sin to to kill them.' Smuggling was also a 'social crime' (see box). Juries would not convict a smuggler and whole communities of people did not regard smuggling as a crime at all (Source 5).

After the Poole Customs House raid and the murder of Chater in 1747 the Duke of Richmond tried to smash the smuggling gangs. He was given a special Commission to do so in 1748, with outsiders as magistrates and judges, and £100 reward for information. As a result 35 smugglers were hanged and 10 more died in gaol.

However, there was still too much money to be made for smuggling to die out. The public were too keen on their cheap 'black market' smuggled tea or brandy. The real decline of smuggling came with the removal of import duties. In 1784 Prime Minister William Pitt the Younger cut the duty on tea from 119% to 12.5%. Further reductions took place in the early 19th century and the heyday of smuggling was over.

**✶✶✶✶✶✶✶✶✶✶✶✶✶✶✶✶✶✶✶✶✶✶✶✶✶✶✶✶✶✶✶✶✶✶✶✶✶✶**

### Social crime

Historians use this term to describe crimes that large numbers of people do not think of as crimes. In the 18th century many people regarded smuggling as a lawful way of making a living and the government import duties as stupid, deserving to be broken. Other 'social crimes' were poaching and, in some places, wrecking (see pages 114–115).

**✶✶✶✶✶✶✶✶✶✶✶✶✶✶✶✶✶✶✶✶✶✶✶✶✶✶✶✶✶✶✶✶✶✶✶✶✶✶**

❖ *In what ways did governments create the crime of smuggling?*
❖ *Was smuggling a 'social crime'?*
❖ *What goods do modern-day smugglers carry?*
❖ *Do you regard modern-day smuggling as a 'social crime'?*

# HIGHWAYMEN

*KEY QUESTION*
◆ *Do highwaymen deserve to be heroes?*

In the 16th, 17th and 18th centuries highway robbery was quite a common crime. Travellers were in real danger of being robbed, which is why so many people went about armed. In Essex in the reign of Queen Elizabeth, for example, there were 129 murders, 320 robberies, 1,460 other thefts and 110 cases of highway robbery. Even Oliver Cromwell was robbed on the highway. Source 1 shows the Earl of Eglinton being robbed.

## Why were the roads unsafe?

Read Source 2 for evidence of these three factors in the case of John Evelyn, in 1652:

● The population was much smaller, with fewer built-up areas. Roads often went through quiet, lonely countryside. There were plenty of places for highway robbers to hide. There were also far fewer travellers, so highway robbers could carry out their crimes without being interrupted.

### SOURCE 1

Highwaymen robbing the Earl of Eglinton at Hounslow, June 1750.

### SOURCE 2

The weather being hot, I sent my servant ahead and rode slowly in the shade. Within three miles of Bromley two cut-throats armed with sticks sprang out and, striking at the horse and taking hold of the reins, threw me down and took my sword. They hauled me into a deep thicket some quarter of a mile from the highway in order to rob me. They took quite a lot of money, but they also took two rings, one an emerald with diamonds, and a buckle set with rubies and diamonds.

They bound my hands and feet, having before pulled off my boots. They tied my horse to a tree but let him graze.

Left in this way I was tormented with flies, ants and the sun. After two hours trying I got the cord over my wrist, unbound my feet, saddled my horse and found the highway. The next morning, sore as my wrists were, I went to London and got 500 notices printed and sent out. Within two days I had news of all I had lost, except my sword.

*John Evelyn is robbed on the highway near Bromley in June 1652.*

● There were fewer banks, no credit cards or cheques, so people carried their wealth around with them, as cash or jewels.

● As we have seen in Chapter 2, there was no police force to prevent crime or to chase criminals once a crime had been committed. Highway robbers therefore stood a good chance of getting away with it.

## Footpads and highwaymen

Strictly speaking, the men who robbed John Evelyn in Source 2 were footpads. That is, they were on foot, not on horseback. Footpads did not usually try to rob mounted travellers because they could escape more easily. A highwayman, mounted on a horse, could hold up richer victims, who were in coaches or on horseback themselves. With the chance of making quite a lot of money it is perhaps not surprising that there were plenty of highwaymen.

## Why are highwaymen seen as heroes?

There are a number of myths about highwaymen. To start with, a highwayman rode a horse, and to ride a horse put you above low, violent criminals like footpads. Highwaymen were therefore supposed to behave better:

- They were supposed only to rob the rich and to help the poor.
- They were supposed to be well-mannered and to refuse to rob women.
- They were supposed to dress well, like the better off people who were their victims.

These myths were popular at the time when real highwaymen roamed the roads. The most popular play of the 18th century, *The Beggar's Opera*, which opened in 1725, starred a handsome highwayman called MacHeath.

### SOURCE 3

*James MacLean described himself as a 'Gentleman Highwayman'. In a letter to a newspaper in 1764 he said he had:*

Made a couple of sneaking footpads give back the money, a week's wages, they had taken from a poor labourer.

### SOURCE 4

*Claude Duval, a Frenchman, was hanged for highway robbery in 1670. His tombstone has this poem:*

Here lies Duval. Reader, if male thou art,
Look to thy purse: if female, to thy heart.

### SOURCE 5

*The Newgate Calendar described the lives, and deaths, of prisoners in Newgate Prison, London. One 18th-century highwayman it described was Thomas Butler:*

There are few highwaymen who lived in such elegance as Butler. He used to dress in black velvet, laced ruffles and all the other clothes of a gentleman.

### SOURCE 6

PHILIP FRIEND · CHARLES COBURN
WANDA HENDRIX
CECIL KELLAWAY · VICTOR JORY
SCOTT FORBES · VIRGINIA HUSTON
DAN O'HERLIHY · HENRY MORGAN
ALBERT SHARPE · ALAN NAPIER
AN ALLIED ARTISTS PICTURE
COLOUR BY CINECOLOR
The Highwayman

Film poster from the 1950s.

When highwaymen disappeared, the myths lingered on. In 1825 a popular poem made Dick Turpin the most famous highwaymen of all time. He was supposed to have escaped the law by riding his horse, Black Bess, from London to York in one day. Even in the 20th century the idea of the highwayman, a lone figure calling on a rich traveller to 'Stand and Deliver! Your money or your life!' has inspired films (Source 6) and many stories.

---

### DICK TURPIN

The real Dick Turpin was born in Essex in 1705. He was trained as a butcher in London, but turned to cattle-stealing. He then joined a gang of violent house-breakers. In 1735, at Loughton, Essex, their victim, a widow, would not tell them where she had hidden her money. Turpin is reported to have threatened to put her on the fire and said: 'God damn your blood, you old bitch, if you won't tell me I'll set your arse on the grate.'

When some of the gang were arrested and hanged he turned to highway robbery, with a friend called Tom King. They lived in a cave in Epping Forest. He became too well-known in Essex so in 1737 he went to Yorkshire. He changed his name and took up horse-stealing. For this he was hanged at York in 1739.

He never owned a horse called Black Bess, nor rode from London to York. Someone who did carry out a ride like this was a robber called Nevison. He robbed a man in Kent, then rode to York in 16 hours, at a time when the stage-coach took three days, so that it would appear that he could not have been in Kent when the crime was committed.

---

1. *What does Source 2 tell us about law and order in the 17th century?*
2. *How far do Sources 3, 4 and 5, and the information in the box on Dick Turpin support the popular myths about highwaymen?*
3. *Use these sources and your knowledge to explain why highwaymen were popular heroes.*
4. *Use these sources and your own knowledge to comment on the accuracy of the image of a highwayman in Source 6.*
5. *Why have highwaymen disappeared?*

# INDUSTRIAL BRITAIN

| | |
|---|---|
| **1750** | 1750s Sir John Fielding sets up Bow Street Runners |
| | 1777 John Howard's report on prisons |
| | 1798 River Thames Police founded |
| **1800** | |
| | 1812 Luddite riots |
| | 1815 Battle of Waterloo, end of Napoleonic Wars |
| | 1816 Elizabeth Fry begins work at Newgate Prison |
| | 1819 Peterloo massacre |
| **1820** | |
| | 1823 Gaols Act |
| | 1825 Opening of Stockton and Darlington steam railway |
| | 1829 Metropolitan Police Act |
| | 1830 Captain Swing riots |
| | 1832 Great Reform Act |
| | 1834 Tolpuddle Martyrs |
| | 1837 Publication of *Oliver Twist* by Charles Dickens |
| | 1839 First Chartist petition |
| **1840** | 1843 Peak of Rebecca riots in Wales |
| | 1848 Third Chartist petition |
| | 1851 By this date the majority of British people lived in urban areas |
| | 1854 Reformatory schools for offenders under 16 |
| | 1856 County Borough Police Act |
| **1860** | |
| | 1865 Prisons Act: 'hard labour, hard food, hard board' |
| | 1868 Abolition of public hanging |
| | 1877 CID started |
| **1880** | |
| | 1889 London Dock Strike |
| | 1890 Police Act: proper careers for policemen |
| | 1898 Prisons Act based on Gladstone Report |
| **1900** | |

## Industry

In this period Britain changed from being a mainly agricultural economy to a mainly industrial one. Factory production and new technology led to an enormous increase in production of coal, iron, steel, cotton and other manufactured goods, sold across the world. There were spectacular improvements in transport, with 23,000 miles of railway built by 1900.

## People

People's lives changed dramatically. Millions moved from rural areas to work in the new industries in towns and cities. New huge cities grew up. Population increased from 11 million in 1750 to 42 million by 1900. Life in these new cities was tough, especially in the early 19th century. Working conditions were hard, housing was unhealthy and overcrowded. Employment was uncertain and workers could be laid off with little notice and nothing to live on.

## Government

These enormous industrial, economic and social changes were not met by changes in the way the country was run. Britain in the early 19th century was the most modern economy in the world, with a 17th-century system of government. Change did come, but it had to be struggled for.

# CRIME IN INDUSTRIAL BRITAIN

*KEY QUESTIONS*
◆ *How did crime change?*
◆ *What factors caused these changes?*

Figures for crimes committed were not collected until 1805, so historians have to estimate crime figures for years before that, often using local records. Using crime statistics is full of problems anyway (see Chapter 5), so we should be aware that the figures here are far from reliable.

The general picture for the period covered by this chapter was a gradual increase in crime from 1750 to the early 19th century, then a dramatic rise up to about 1840, then a gradual decline. The period of most rapid rise in crime (about 25 years) is shown in Source 1.

There were new crimes, created by new laws, such as obstructing a police officer, or failing to send your children to school. In many ways crime did not change: 90% of crimes were crimes against property, of which by far the most common, as always, was small-scale theft. Pickpockets, like the Parsons (Source 2), were not that different from the petty criminals who had flourished for centuries. The only difference might be that, in the past, if they were spotted, the crowd would beat them up a bit, throw them in the pond, and forget it. Now they had been arrested, tried, photographed, imprisoned and had become a criminal statistic. Three-quarters of all criminals were males, with the numbers of females involved in crime declining throughout the period.

The enormous changes which took place in Britain during this period were bound to have an impact on the

**SOURCE 1**

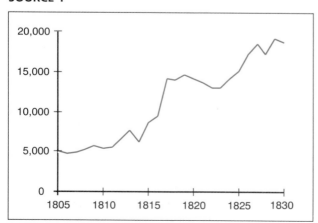

Number of recorded crimes per year in the early 19th century.

**SOURCE 2**

A husband and wife pickpocket team: Thomas and Louisa Parsons, photographed in Derby gaol in 1865.

nature of crime. More trade and industry gave more opportunities for stealing, from shops, factories, ships, warehouses, wagons, barges and trains. Many people were better off, giving richer pickings to thieves. Cities were larger, with bigger crowds of people whose pockets could be picked.

Highway robbery died out as roads became less isolated, with more traffic, more patrols and more turnpike gates. A new crime was robbing travellers on the railway, especially before the introduction of corridor trains. Huge new business ventures, operating with minimum supervision, provided rich opportunities for crooked dealings. Many investors lost money in the 1840s railway fraud scandal, for example. In 1882 over £1 million was embezzled from Jardine Matheson and in 1897 millions were embezzled from Baring Brothers bank (both crimes were hushed up).

## Reasons for the increase in crime

**1. Population.** Crime rates, even when the figures are reliable, have to be related to population: more people could mean more crime without looking for any other factors. Certainly the population rose spectacularly: from 11 million in 1750, to 16 million in 1800, to 27 million in 1850 to 42 million in 1900. Although people at the time did not know it, population increases probably accounted for most of the rise in crime from 1750 to about 1810. However, it cannot account for the rise shown in Source 1.

**2. Poverty.** The ruling classes rarely like to admit it, but poverty can cause crime. Source 1 shows that the steep rise in crime was erratic. Its peaks coincided with times of greatest hardship and distress. For example, the years of greatest increase on the graph are the years just after the long Napoleonic wars ended in 1815. They were hard years, with industry finding it difficult to adjust to peace and thousands of ex-soldiers looking for work (see also 'Protest: Peterloo', page 78).

Historians also point to individual evidence like the two examples in Source 3. They note that small thefts in these bad years were often committed by men in their late 20s and 30s. It is rare for first offenders to come from this age-group: perhaps they are unemployed factory workers stealing for their families.

**3. Drink.** Many people in 19th-century Britain saw alcohol as the root of all kinds of evil, from the break-up of the family to the increase in crime (Source 4). Certainly some crimes were committed to get money to feed alcohol addiction. Those who lost their jobs through being drunk may have turned to crime. Pubs were also places where criminals met. But this does not really explain why people turned to drink, or why pubs were so attractive (Source 5).

## SOURCE 3

*Poverty and crime:*

**A** In Bedfordshire in 1819 Thomas Parkins stole firewood from the Honourable William Waldergrave: 'I was in great distress, my wife near lying-in, I went to get firewood to make her a bit of a fire.'

**B** In Leicestershire in 1822 John Stone stole a watch: 'I am a poor stocking-weaver in distress. I was travelling to Leicester, having been to London to offer myself as a soldier, but I was not tall enough. My parents are in distress, my father out of work; I have eight brothers and sisters.'

## SOURCE 4

In every shape and form, from theft, fraud and prostitution in the young, to burnings, robberies, and more hardened offences in the old, an enormous mass of human beings, who under sober habits and moral training would be sources of wealth and strength to the country, are transformed under the influence of Intoxicating Drink.

*Parliament blames drink for the crime wave, 1834.*

## SOURCE 5

A London street corner on a Sunday morning, 1856.

**4. City life.** By 1851 a majority of the British population lived in urban areas. Most of them, however, were migrants: they had been born in rural areas and moved to cities to seek work. City life was very different from what they had been used to. Living conditions were often squalid: overcrowded, unhealthy and expensive. New arrivals were often alone, without the support of the village or small town community they had known all their lives.

In this situation it is not surprising that some turned to the pub, with its bright lights, glittering mirrors, comfort and easy companionship. And that is as far as it went, for most of them: a refuge from the ghastly housing they had to rent. For some others, however, it was a small step to crime. The poorest housing which new arrivals had to take was often the home of criminals too; the network of criminals offered the country boy or girl instant friendship; pub acquaintances offered a more glamorous lifestyle. Then the work itself might suddenly come to an end, leaving nothing to live on, or they felt the need for a bit of extra cash. Your first crime was then all too easy.

❖ *In what ways was crime in industrial Britain different from crime in the 17th and early 18th centuries?*

❖ *List the features of early 19th-century city life which led people to turn to crime.*
 *(i) Group these into: economic; social; personal.*
 *(ii) Write a paragraph on each, explaining how important each factor was in causing crime.*

*KEY QUESTIONS*
◆ *What did people at the time think of the crime situation?*

## Popular interest

People in 19th-century Britain were very interested in crime. At the popular level there were newspapers devoted entirely to reporting recent crimes, in lurid detail (Source 6). There were few restrictions on reporting, and using artists to draw scenes from the crime allowed them to print the kinds of pictures we are not allowed to show as photographs today. Charles Dickens used his intimate knowledge of London to thrill his readers by publishing novels and articles about London's criminal underworld (Source 7). Detective novels, like *The Adventures of Sherlock Holmes*, published in 1891, were eagerly read.

Madame Tussauds opened in 1802, and had popular waxworks of criminals, particularly murderers. Murder featured a great deal, perhaps as it was, after the 1860s, the only offence carrying the death penalty. There was huge interest in celebrated 19th-century horror crimes, like the Ratcliffe Highway murders of

**SOURCE 6**

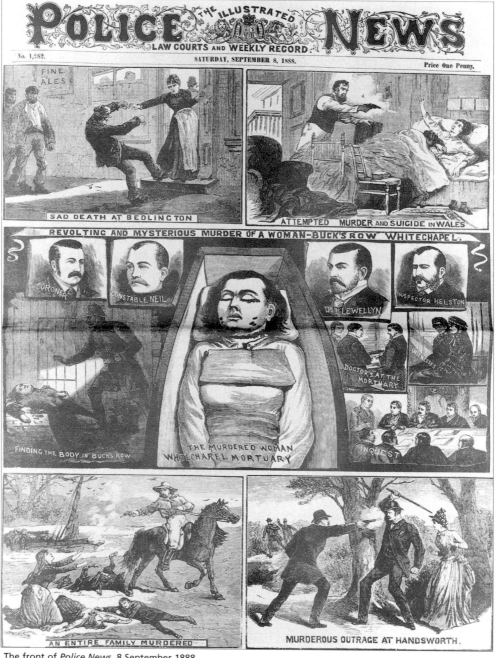

The front of *Police News*, 8 September 1888.

1811, in which two families were battered to death, and the 'Jack the Ripper' murders of 1888. The statistics, however, show that numbers of murders were static at about 400 a year. Then, as now, most murders took place in the family.

Popular interest could, in fact, create a crime wave. In July 1863 an MP, Hugh Pilkington, was garrotted and robbed in central London. This led to a 'garrotting scare': there were 12 more recorded cases in October and 32 in November. Maybe the press reports of the original case led criminals to copy the tactic. Maybe the police or the public labelled certain kinds of robbery 'garrottings' which they would not have done before.

## SOURCE 7

We stoop low and creep down a steep flight of steps into a dark close cellar. There is a fire. There is a long deal table. There are benches. The cellar is full of company, chiefly very young men in various conditions of dirt and raggedness. Some are eating supper. There are no girls or women present. Welcome to Rat's Castle, gentlemen, and to this company of noted thieves!

*Charles Dickens describes a visit made with 'Inspector Field'.*

## SOURCE 8

Hot as the place was, most of the women wore shawls about their heads. They were coarse-looking and repulsive – more than one with bloodshot and discoloured faces. The men were of that class you often notice in low areas – squalid hulking fellows with no particular mark of any trade upon them. The women were of the worst class of prostitutes, and the men their bullies and partners in robberies.

*In an article in the* Morning Chronicle, *Angus Reach describes a visit with a police inspector to a lodging-house in Angel Meadow, Manchester.*

## SOURCE 9

*In the fourth volume of* London Labour and the London Poor, 1861–62, *Mayhew describes over 100 different types of criminal, including:*

Till friskers, who empty tills while the shopman is away;

Sawney-hunters, who steal bacon from cheesemongers' shop-doors;

Noisy-racket men, who steal china and glass from outside china shops;

Dead lurkers, who steal coats and umbrellas from passages at dusk or on Sunday afternoons;

Snow-gatherers, who steal clean clothes off hedges.

## Criminal types

A sort of science grew up which claimed that there was a recognisable 'criminal type' which could be recognised by certain physical features. The doctor at Perth prison took measurements of the inmates' skulls, and insisted they showed distinct characteristics. A schoolteacher who worked at Newgate Prison in 1830 claimed the prisoners had 'animal' features.

The middle and upper classes were fairly terrified of the new phenomenon: the industrial city. The sections on Protest in this chapter (see pages 77–85) give some idea of the class conflict of this period.

Given the rise of the city and the rise in crime many writers formed the idea that there was a 'criminal class'. These were people who had chosen a life of crime in preference to working. They were to be found in cities, and various writers tried to describe them. The most famous and detailed of these descriptions was by Henry Mayhew, who, with a team of helpers, set out to define and describe London's poor. In Source 9 he lists some of the kinds of criminals he has unearthed in a section he calls 'the non-workers, or dangerous classes, of the metropolis.' Charles Booth later (1902) grouped 'occasional labourers, loafers and semi-criminals' in the same class.

Certainly there were areas of towns and cities where large numbers of the people lived by crime. In London there were the 'rookeries': narrow streets of old, run-down properties, with alleyways between them and interconnecting cellars. They offered a hideaway to criminals and those on the fringes of the law. The largest rookery in London was at St Giles, at the eastern end of Oxford Street, before it was pulled down to create New Oxford Street in the middle of the century. Jacob's Island, in Charles Dickens' *Oliver Twist* and the Jago in Arthur Harding's *Child of the Jago* are fictional versions of these kinds of areas.

However, a few habitual criminals in some areas do not make a class. The fact that most criminals who came before the courts were from the poorest sections of the working class does not mean that that class was criminal. There were plenty of poor working-class people who were not habitual criminals.

❖ *Why did middle-class investigators think that they had found a 'criminal class'?*
❖ *What is wrong with this theory of the cause of crime?*

# THE FIELDINGS AND CRIME PREVENTION IN THE LATE 18TH CENTURY

## KEY QUESTION

◆ *What did people in the later 18th century think should be done about crime?*

Law enforcement in the 18th century was the same as it had been for centuries: the old Anglo-Saxon system of getting everyone to serve as constable for a year still existed. The watchmen still operated under laws passed by Charles II, and so were called 'Charleys'. They were widely regarded as almost useless at preventing crime or catching criminals (Source 1). Official crime prevention was so bad that groups of shopkeepers grouped together to carry out their own schemes, a bit like today's 'Neighbourhood Watch'. Many town JPs were corrupt, selling licences and arrest warrants. If someone committed a crime against you, you still had to prosecute him or her in court yourself. This was expensive and time-consuming and in some places 'Societies for Prosecuting Felons' were set up to bear these costs.

When people thought about serious crime in Britain in the years after 1750 they thought about London crime. London was already the largest city in Europe at that time, with over half a million people and rising fast. At the centre of law enforcement in London for over 30 years between them were two half-brothers, Henry and John Fielding.

## SOURCE 1

The beats of many watchmen are so short that they take only five minutes to walk them; which, done twice in an hour, means that he is either fifty minutes in his box or, what is more frequent, they meet two or three together in conversation. Frequently they are employed in shutting up shops, or going on errands for the inhabitants or going into public houses with prostitutes. Also, from their practice of being fixed in a certain box for many years, there is no doubt some of them receive bribes from persons who commit robberies.

*Matthew Wood, Lord Mayor of London.*

## SOURCE 2

Whoever considers the cities of London and Westminster, with the late vast addition of their suburbs, the immense number of lanes, alleys, courts and byplaces, must think that, had they been intended for the very purpose of concealment, they could scarce have been better contrived.

*From Henry Fielding's* Enquiry into the Late Increase in Robbers, *1751.*

## SOURCE 3

Sir John Fielding.

## Henry Fielding

Henry Fielding was a novelist who took on the paid post of London's main magistrate at Bow Street in 1748. On the basis of what he saw of London crime he wrote his *Enquiry into the Late Increase in Robbers*, in 1751. It was one of the first attempts in Britain to analyse the causes of crime. He put the blame for the increase in crime on the breakdown of order and hard work among the people who flocked to London hoping to make an easy living. He also blamed the government for being corrupt and so setting a bad example. He said that conditions in London led people into a life of crime (Source 2). He also tried to make some practical changes. He could see that of the 80 constables in his area only six were any good. When their turn ended he persuaded them to stay on and help him to break up some of London's criminal gangs.

Henry Fielding also began a magazine called the *Covent Garden Journal* to pass on information about crimes and criminals. This kind of publicity was very useful at a time when each wronged person had to do their own police-work and bring their own prosecution. When he retired in 1754 his place was taken by his half-brother John.

## Sir John Fielding

Sir John was blind (Source 3); but from his long service as magistrate (1754–80), he was said to be able to recognise 3,000 London criminals from their voices alone. Under his guidance, Bow Street became more like a police station and his efficient, trained and paid constables made the streets of London safer. They began to be called the Bow Street Runners (Source 4). He published details of crimes and criminals on the front page of the Monday edition of a London newspaper.

He put forward several plans for catching thieves and preventing crime:

**(a) 1755:** 'A Plan for Preventing Robberies within Twenty Miles of London'. People living around London would join together and pay a subscription. This would be used to pay a special troop of mounted men. If a crime was committed they would go straight to Bow Street with the details which would be circulated throughout London. The idea was not taken up.

**(b) 1763:** London to be divided into six areas, each with a police station and paid patrols like the Bow Street Runners. The idea was not taken up. However, part of the plan was for patrols on the main roads into London. The government gave him £600 to hire eight men to carry out these patrols. They virtually put an end to highway robbery, so the government money was stopped. The highwaymen returned!

**(c) 1772–73:** 'The General Preventative Plan'. This was a plan to extend some of the crime prevention Henry and he had carried out in London to the whole country. He called on all JPs and gaolers to supply him with details of all crimes committed and criminals convicted. The government gave him £400 to put all this together and publish it in a news-sheet called the *Hue and Cry*. JPs and mayors were asked to display this in their areas. It was the beginning of a national crime information network.

**(d) 1775:** All high constables within 160 kilometres of London were to live on the main road. They would chase offenders and were given money to pay for a horse. The number of constables was also to be increased. This plan failed: high constables considered themselves too important to live by the roadside. They were also reluctant to do London's thief-catching.

John Townshend, a Bow Street Runner.

It might seem that Henry and John Fielding had only limited success. Certainly there was still strong opposition to anything like a police force (see next page), and to raising the money to pay for it. However, in 1792 London was divided into seven police districts, each with three magistrates and six paid constables. In 1798 the River Thames Police was set up. By 1800 there were 68 Bow Street Runners (Source 4). In 1805 54 men were taken on to patrol the main roads, armed with pistol, cutlass and truncheon. They were nicknamed 'Robin Redbreasts' from their red waistcoats.

❖ *Why was law and order in London in the late 18th century breaking down?*
❖ *How did Sir John Fielding's various schemes raise the money they needed to work?*
❖ *Why were all his plans to widen crime prevention beyond Bow Street ineffective in his lifetime?*

# REFORM OF THE POLICE

*KEY QUESTIONS*
◆ *Is the story of police reform one of steady progress?*
◆ *Why did people object to the setting up of police forces?*

Well into the 19th century, the policing of Britain was, as in so many things, old-fashioned, patchy and mostly inadequate. London had only 450 constables and 4,000 watchmen to police a population in excess of 1,500,000. Liverpool's population was 250,000, policed by just 50 watchmen. Newcastle, however, had an efficient system of police sergeants and constables, under the control of the Mayor and corporation.

A common interpretation of the story of the setting up of police all over Britain is that it was a steady progress, from Bow Street Runners (see page 65) via the Metropolitan Police, to a national force. Anyone who opposed this development was either stupid or wicked. As you read these pages, look at how steady this development was.
● Did one system simply copy the one before?
● Who controlled the police in each case?
● Were the objections stupid or wicked?

The two main objections to setting up a police force were:

(a) It wasn't the government's business to do things like this. If people wanted a police force they would get together and start one themselves. It would be cheaper and under local control.

(b) There was a long-standing fear that a police force could be used by the government like an army, to arrest opponents, and crush free speech and democracy. This was linked to the usual British dislike of anything foreign (Source 1). There was tremendous hostility to the undemocratic government of the time, see page 77. The government employed spies and soldiers were used to crush a demonstration at Peterloo in 1819 (see page 78), causing a great outcry.

## The Metropolitan Police Act, 1829

Sir Robert Peel, Home Secretary, decided that crime was increasing so fast, especially in London, that something had to be done. The Metropolitan Police Act set up a police force for London. It covered an area up to 7 miles (11 km) from the centre, extended to 15 miles (24 km) in 1839. There were 17 divisions, each with four inspectors and 144 constables.

## SOURCE 1

They have admirable police in Paris, but they pay for it dear enough. I had rather half a dozen men's throats should be cut in Radcliffe Highway every 3 or 4 years than be subject to house raids, spies and all the rest of it.

*An MP opposes the introduction of police, 1811.*

**SOURCE 2**

'Peelers' making an arrest in a cheap lodging house, 1848.

It was run by two Commissioners: an ex-soldier, Colonel Charles Rowan, and a lawyer, Richard Mayne. It was responsible direct to the Home Secretary. The constables (called 'Peelers', after the Home Secretary), had a uniform chosen to look as un-soldierly as possible (Source 2).

They were not an instant success. Many of the first 2,800 recruits were unsuitable: 2,200 were sacked or resigned. Many people, rich and poor alike, bitterly resented them (Source 3). Some drove their coaches straight at policemen on traffic duty. JPs disliked the fact that they were under the Home Secretary's control, not theirs, and were hostile to the police in court. The worst case of hostility was in 1833, when PC Culley was stabbed to death in a political demonstration and his attacker was acquitted by the jury, who were all given medals. After a while, however, people did begin to appreciate that their presence made a difference to the amount of crime, although Source 4 exaggerates this.

## What about the rest of Britain?

**The Municipal Corporations Act, 1835**, set up 178 new boroughs. If they wished, they could have a police force, under the control of the borough Watch Committee.

**SOURCE 3**
Anti-Police
cartoon, 1832.

THE POLICE FORCE ON DUTY.

**SOURCE 4**

There has been a great lessening of the amount of crime committed in London, since the setting up of the new police. The great organisations of criminals have been broken up and scattered in all directions.

*J. Grant, writing in 1836.*

**Rural Constabulary Act, 1839**. There was discussion, in 1839, of extending the London system to the counties, but many people were against it, for all the reasons given above. In the end, the Act permitted the 54 counties of England, if they wished, to set up a county police force under the control of local magistrates.

You can see that both these Acts were 'permissive': that is, they permitted, but did not compel. In fact, even by the 1850s several boroughs still did not have a police force, and some were very small: Bedford had nine policemen and Horncastle, in Lincolnshire, two. At the same time only 36 counties had police forces, and some of these did not cover the whole county. Many rural areas objected to the cost (Source 5). 25% of rural police were privately employed by rich people simply to protect their own property.

**SOURCE 5**

The parish of Harworth has paid during the last year £21-9-2 (£21.46p) as their quota of the expenses of maintaining the County Constabulary without receiving any benefit whatsoever.

*The village of Harworth, Nottinghamshire, objects to paying for the county police, 1843.*

Nevertheless, it was this system, with police under the control of local magistrates, dealing with all kinds of local laws, that was the model for police forces in rural Britain.

**The County Borough Police Act, 1856** compelled all counties and boroughs to have a police force, under joint control of magistrates and councillors. 239 forces were set up. They varied enormously in details, especially over the wages, hours and conditions of work (see page 120).

Three national Inspectors of Police tried to ensure some sort of national standard. Forces they judged 'efficient' received a government grant of 25% towards their costs. In 1856 only 120 forces were found to be efficient, but by 1890 all of them passed.

❖ *What were the differences between the Bow Street Runners and the Metropolitan Police?*
❖ *What were the differences between the Metropolitan Police and the new Borough and County forces?*
❖ *Use these differences, and the time-lag between the changes, to decide whether 19th-century police reform was steady progress.*
❖ *How important was central government in carrying out these reforms?*

# PUNISHMENT IN THE 18TH CENTURY: TRANSPORTATION AND PRISONS

## KEY QUESTIONS

◆ *How had punishments changed by the late 18th century?*

By the 18th century, some of the more savage physical punishments of the Tudor period were rarely used. People were still whipped (public whipping of women stopped in 1817), but branding, ear-slicing and nose-slitting had ceased. Also in decline were those punishments, such as the stocks and the pillory, remnants of a much earlier era, which really involved handing over the criminal to the public to punish. This was partly because they no longer worked: some of those pilloried lost an eye, or were even killed; some wore armour to protect themselves. On the other hand, someone like the bookseller John Williams, who sold papers criticising the government in 1765, was cheered and raised £200 in a collection.

We saw on page 51 that, despite the so-called Bloody Code, judges and juries were reluctant to see criminals hanged. They therefore needed another severe punishment, more serious than a whipping.

**SOURCE 1**

A former warship used as a prison hulk, mid-19th century. These hulks were rotten, insanitary – the worst prison conditions in Britain. Prisoners were kept in irons most of the time because they were overcrowded, and had a 25% mortality rate.

## Transportation

For two centuries, from 1654 to 1857, this was provided by 'transporting' convicts to the colonies, for periods of seven or 14 years, or life. Between 1717 and 1776, 30,000 convicts were transported to Virginia, Maryland or the Caribbean. As with gaols, transportation was run as a business. For example, Stephenson and Randolph, of Bristol, described themselves as 'felon-dealers'. They arranged the transport of convicts and sold them to the Caribbean plantations for up to £80 each.

When the USA became independent in 1776 they obviously refused to take any more British convicts. Then, from 1788, transportation to Australia began. Australia had only been mapped and claimed for Britain in 1770 and the government was keen to make its claim stronger by settling the new colony. Over the next 65 years, 150,000 people were sent to Australia; only one in eight of them were women. They were sent for trivial offences: stealing goods worth 1/- (5p), or stealing fish from someone's pond. A nine-year-old, John Inskip, was sentenced to be transported for seven years for stealing 2/2 (11p). Many of those transported were really political prisoners: those who took part in Luddism, Captain Swing riots, Rebecca riots and Chartism. Most famous of all were the Tolpuddle Martyrs, sentenced to transportation in 1834 for trying to form a trade union. (For all these protest movements, see pages 80–85 and 112–115.)

Those awaiting transportation were put in the 'hulks': disused warships (Source 1). Conditions on the convict ships themselves were appalling (Source 2). The journey took six months, and many died on the way. Once in Australia, some were kept in barracks and worked the land. Others were sent to work for free settlers. Some of these were treated quite well and, once you had served your time, you could make a new life. Sentencing to transportation ended in 1857, mainly as a result of pressure from the colonies.

Conditions below deck on a transportation ship going to Australia, mid-19th century.

## Prisons and houses of correction

By the 18th century many more offenders than before, some 60% of those convicted, received a 'custodial' sentence, i.e. they were locked up. For petty offenders, many JPs favoured sending them to the House of Correction, rather than prison. These had been set up to deal with the able-bodied poor (see page 43), and were based on the principle of making the inmates work. Those who sent them there seem to have hoped that the discipline of work would reform young, or first offenders.

Prisons in this period were awful places.
● All kinds of prisoners were thrown in together: convicts, those awaiting trial, lunatics, debtors, women and children.

● They were very unhealthy, damp, overcrowded, and insanitary, with no toilets, running water or sewage system. Many old castles were still used as gaols, relics from an earlier time. 'Gaol-fever', as it was called (probably dysentery or typhus), killed many of the inmates. In 1577, at the Oxford Assizes, several jurymen and two of the judges caught gaol-fever and died.

● Your life in prison depended on the personality of the gaoler. English governments were obsessed with not having too many officials paid for by the public, so gaolers ran their prisons as businesses (Source 3). This meant that you could have a reasonable time if you had money: you could buy your own room, good food and drink, and your friends and family were allowed to visit. Poor prisoners depended on local charities paying their fees.

Historians know more about Newgate Gaol then any other, because, being in London, it was more written about. No doubt other gaols were similar. A room on the 'Master Side' cost £3 6s 8d (£3.33p) a week. The charity wards were grossly overcrowded, built for 150 prisoners, but containing 275. The day began at 7 a.m., when the bell clanged, prisoners' leg-irons were unlocked and they saw to their own washing and breakfast. They were largely left alone by the warders until 9 p.m. when they were locked up again. Inmates elected their own 'Steward' and 'Wardsmen' to run the place.

Anything was allowed, if you tipped the gaoler. Some prisoners kept pets; ale and tobacco could be bought – the gaoler estimated that he made £400 a year from brewing his own ale to sell; prostitutes sometimes visited. There was a chapel, but ministers complained of bad behaviour – laughing, yawning, coughing – during the services. The last sermon preached to a prisoner who was going to be hanged was a special occasion: the gaolers would sell tickets, at £20 each, to the public, to hear it.

### SOURCE 3

| | |
|---|---|
| Admission fee | 3s 0d (15p) |
| Release fee | 6s 10d (34p) |
| Sharing a bed with another prisoner | 1s 3d (6p) a week |
| Bed to yourself | 2s 6d (12 1/2p) a week |

*Fees charged by the gaoler at Newgate prison, in 1729.*

### **********PUNISHMENT BOX**********

#### Transportation

The main purpose of this was to remove people from society. Its deterrent effect was weakened because few people knew exactly what happened to people who were transported.

#### Prisons

There was, then as now, some conflict over the purposes of prison. It certainly kept criminals out of society. Some felt its purpose was to deter others from turning to crime. Others wanted to reform convicted criminals through making them work.

**********************************

❖ *What were the **advantages** of transportation? Think about: judges, who had to pass sentence, overcrowded prisons, government, those transported.*
❖ *What were the **disadvantages** of transportation? Think about: the convicts' families, those transported, the feelings of the colonists.*

# PRISON REFORM (1)

## KEY QUESTIONS
◆ *How did prisons change in this period?*
◆ *Why were these changes carried out?*

As with the police, Britain entered the 19th century with a prison system dating back centuries. It was out of date both in the buildings and the way they were run. The government did not even know how many prisons there were in Britain. Look back at the three factors that made prisons so awful given on page 69. What would you do to correct each one? And how would you go about getting things changed?

A number of people devoted their lives to improving prisons. They had two motives.

First, prisons were cruel and unfair: many of the reformers were Christians who pointed out that convicts were God's creatures too. People's lives were being wasted, languishing in gaol when they could change their ways and become decent citizens.

Second, gaols were inefficient: over half of all prisoners were either debtors or had served their sentence but could not afford to pay the gaoler the release fee. It was also obviously not right that someone sentenced to gaol should stand a good chance of dying of typhus.

As you read about these reformers, think not only about **what** they did, but also what their **motives** were and **how** they set about making changes happen.

## SOURCE 1

In some gaols you see boys of 12 and 13 eagerly listening to the stories told by experienced criminals, of their adventures, successes, strategems and escapades.

*John Howard describes one of the effects of mixing all prisoners up together.*

## SOURCE 2

The sallow faces declare, without words, that they are very miserable; many who went in healthy, are, in a few months, changed to emaciated dejected objects. Some are seen expiring on the floors, in loathsome cells, of fevers and smallpox.

*John Howard describes Newgate Gaol in his book* The State of the Prisons in England and Wales, *1777.*

## SOURCE 3

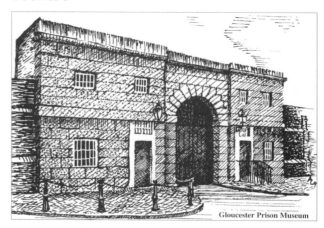

Gloucester Gaol, built for Sir George O. Paul, designed by William Blackburn.

## John Howard

John Howard became High Sheriff of Bedfordshire in 1773. One of his jobs was to inspect the county's gaols and he was shocked by what he saw. He made it his life's work to visit and report on every prison, first in England and Wales, then all of Europe. He was scrupulously careful in his work, measuring each cell, weighing prisoners' food, noting numbers and types of prisoners and recording deaths from disease.

His report on England and Wales came out in 1777 (see Sources 1 and 2). You can see that he didn't mince words, but he did not actually condemn those responsible: local magistrates. They could not argue with his statistics but were not publicly blamed so they could appear to support reform. Howard recommended more space, better food, paid gaolers, separation of types and genders of prisoners. Who would put these ideas into practice?

## Sir George Onesiphorus Paul

Sir George Paul became High Sheriff of Gloucester in 1780 and reacted to his local prisons with much the same disgust as Howard. Howard's report on Gloucester Gaol was damning and Paul realised he could not alter it but would have to build a new one. The Gloucestershire Act, 1785, gave him the powers to do this and he worked with an architect, William Blackburn, to turn his ideas into bricks and mortar.

● The new prison had to be secure. The wall was 5.4 metres high with spikes on top. The buildings were arranged so that gaolers could easily see what was going on.

● It had to be healthy. People believed that disease was caused by bad air, so the gaol was built to suck in fresh air through large gateways, with open portcullises (Source 3). The large, heated cells were reached by open balconies. Howard had admired the 'lazarettos' – isolation wards for health checks at the entrances to many Mediterranean ports. Paul put such a ward by the entrance of his gaol.

● Prisoners were separated into those awaiting trial and those convicted, with male and female sections for each.

● Paul paid attention to the rules (the 'regime'), as well as the buildings. There was a paid Governor, a chaplain and a surgeon, who visited the sick each day and inspected every prisoner once a week. Prisoners were to be reformed through work, education and religion. If they could not read they were taught and given religious books. Staff had to keep detailed journals of what prisoners did and said. Prisoners had to wear a yellow and blue uniform and keep clean; they were not allowed to keep pets or play games. They were well-fed and not kept in irons. They spent long periods on their own, thinking about their life of crime. This **separation** of prisoners from each other was later taken further (see page 72), but at Gloucester it was only for the first nine months of your sentence.

Paul's prison and rules became a model for other prisons.

## Elizabeth Fry and female prisons
(see page 106)

## Sir Robert Peel's Gaols Act, 1823

Peel was influenced by Howard and Fry. This Act pulled together several earlier laws and only dealt with 130 prisons in London, the counties and large towns. Prisons had to be secure and healthy. Gaolers had to be paid. Prisoners had to be divided into their different categories and women prisoners had to be looked after by women warders. JPs had to visit their gaols regularly and report to the Quarter Sessions and the government. Paul's ideas on reform through education, religion and work were adopted. So were his rules for the Governor, surgeon and chaplain and their journals. Unfortunately the Act was often ignored. There were only five Inspectors, not appointed until 1835, with limited powers.

## New prisons

The government soon realised what Sir George Paul had realised, that new and better ideas on how to treat prisoners required new prisons. Millbank Prison was opened in 1816; at a cost of £450,000 it was the largest prison in Europe (Source 4). Between 1842 and 1877, 90 new prisons were built in Britain. They were well-built, with large cells (14' x 11'), each with its own wash-basin, toilet and hammock for sleeping. These buildings are still the core of Britain's prison provision.

The reformer Jeremy Bentham also took a great deal of interest in prison design and reform. His aims were not so much Christian humanity but efficiency. He proposed prisons with blocks radiating out from the centre so that a few warders could supervise the whole prison.

He also believed in reform of prisoners through useful work, the results of which could be sold. This way prisons could even be run at a profit. At Durham the prison built up a good business in mats and rugs made by the prisoners. However Bentham's ideas were not as popular as those of other reformers, as you will see on the next page.

**SOURCE 4**

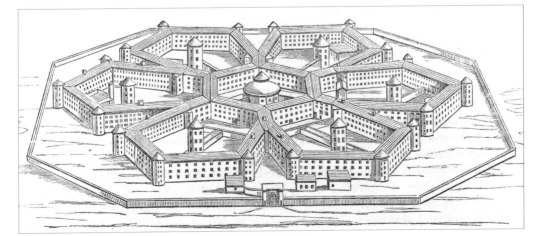

The original design for Millbank Prison.

# PRISON REFORM (2)

**KEY QUESTIONS**

◆ *How did prisons try to reform prisoners?*
◆ *Were prisons better by the late 19th century
than they had been 100 years earlier?*

Britain's leaders in the mid-19th century were full of reforming zeal. They believed they could put anything right: factories, mines, slavery, the police – and prisons. In any period, how you try to change people depends on what you believe about the human personality. During the 19th century these beliefs changed and two different systems were tried in prisons. Both were based on ideas from the USA.

## The Separate System

It was widely believed that the human personality is neutral: what you are like depends on what happens to you. Criminals were bad because they had been open only to wicked influences. If you could expose them only to good influences they will change for the better. 'Good' at that time meant particularly Christianity. This belief had been the basis for Sir George Paul's regime at Gloucester, but it was taken to extremes in the 1840s. Two of the first Prison Inspectors, Crawford and Russell, were convinced by it. Pentonville Prison in London, based on Cherry Hall Penitentiary, Pennsylvania, USA, was run on the 'Separate System'.

In this system prisoners spent nearly all their time in solitary confinement in their cells. Contact with other prisoners was made almost impossible. The chapel was specially designed (Source 5), so that prisoners could see the chaplain but not each other. The chaplain made regular visits to the prisoner, emphasising sinfulness and the need to repent.

Prisoners' uniform included a face-mask and a cap with a large low peak so that prisoners could not recognise or communicate with each other if they met. At exercise time each prisoner held on to a knot on a rope; the knots were at 4.5m intervals, so that prisoners were too far apart to talk. Education and work, which were the other parts of Paul's regime, received less attention under the Separate System.

The effects of a few months of this regime are described in Source 6. It was really mental torture; in its first eight years, 22 prisoners at Pentonville went mad, 26 had serious nervous breakdowns and three committed suicide.

**SOURCE 5**

The Chapel at Wandsworth Prison.

**SOURCE 6**

A few months in the solitary cell renders the prisoner strangely impressible. The chaplain can then make the brawny navvy cry like a child; he can work on his feelings in almost any way he pleases.

*The prison chaplain, the Rev. John Clay, describes the effect of the separate system.*

These results were shocking, and anyway ideas were changing by the middle of the century. More people believed that there was a 'criminal type', even that this type had certain physical characteristics (see page 63). If this was so, then reform was impossible and punishment and deterrence were more important.

Also, with hanging greatly reduced and transportation abolished, prison had become, for the first time, the main form of punishment for British criminals.

## The Silent System

Many believed that prisoners' wills should be broken by a tough regime, which would also be cheaper than the Separate System. The Silent System was based on Auburn Prison, New York. It is particularly associated with the 1865 Prisons Act and the new Assistant Director of Prisons, Sir Edmund du Cane, appointed in 1863, who enforced it.

Prisoners were still confined to their cells for most of their first nine months. They were also forbidden to communicate with other prisoners: there were 11,624 offences against this rule by 1,000 prisoners at Coldbath Fields Prison in one year. Prisoners who committed an offence could be put on a diet of bread and water, or chained up, or whipped. But the main elements of the regime were 'hard labour, hard fare and a hard board.'

**Hard labour.** Gone were Bentham's ideas about useful and saleable work. Hard Labour was intended to be hard and, deliberately, utterly pointless. There were various kinds:

● The treadmill (Source 7). Sometimes the treadmill was harnessed to a mill, but often it just drove weighted air-vanes. Prisoners did ten minutes on and five minutes off for several hours.

● Oakum-picking (Source 8). This involved separating out the fibres from old, tarred ships' ropes so that it could be re-used.

● The crank. This was usually in a prisoner's cell. It was a weighted crank-handle which had a counter on it so that the warder could see how many revolutions the prisoner had made. In some prisons you had to do 1,800 to 'earn' your breakfast, 4,500 for dinner, and so on.

**SOURCE 7**

The treadmill at Coldbath Fields Prison.

**SOURCE 8**

Picking oakum at Coldbath Fields Prison.

● Shot drill. Heavy cannonballs were passed from one to another down a long line of prisoners.

**Hard fare.** The food was deliberately monotonous: breakfast was oatmeal gruel and bread (women got 6oz bread while men got 8oz); dinner was soup and bread on Mondays and Thursdays, meat on Tuesdays and Saturdays and bread and potatoes on Mondays, Wednesdays and Fridays. Supper was the same as breakfast.

**Hard board.** Hard beds replaced hammocks.

## Government control of prisons

The 1865 Prisons Act also abolished the distinction between prisons and houses of correction: 80 smaller prisons were closed, leaving only 113 prisons under local control.

The 1877 Prisons Act put all prisons under Home Office control at last, run by a three-man Prison Commission. 53 smaller prisons were closed.

❖ *Read page 69 again about 18th-century prisons. Make a list of what was wrong with them. How many of these things had been put right by the late 19th century?*
❖ *Make a list of the main features of prison life in the late 19th century.*
❖ *From the prisoners' point of view, which was better: the old system, the Separate System or the Silent System?*
❖ *Which was better from the public's point of view?*

# PRISON REFORM:
# WHY DID IT HAPPEN THEN?

## Class control

Prisons and workhouses, factories and schools all brought the new working classes under control

**RISING CRIME**

worried →

## Middle class and property owners

## Reforming ideas

i) Humanitarians, such as Howard, Fry and Paul
ii) Disciplinarians – the Silent and Separate systems

Marxist interpretation

Reformist interpretation

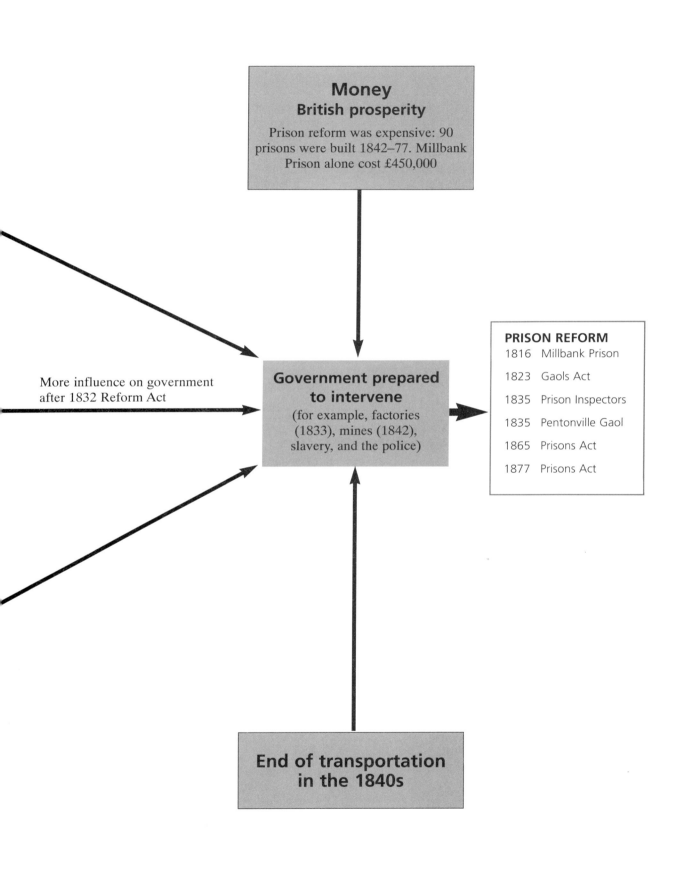

**Money**
**British prosperity**

Prison reform was expensive: 90
prisons were built 1842–77. Millbank
Prison alone cost £450,000

More influence on government
after 1832 Reform Act

**Government prepared
to intervene**
(for example, factories
(1833), mines (1842),
slavery, and the police)

**PRISON REFORM**

| | |
|------|------------------|
| 1816 | Millbank Prison |
| 1823 | Gaols Act |
| 1835 | Prison Inspectors |
| 1835 | Pentonville Gaol |
| 1865 | Prisons Act |
| 1877 | Prisons Act |

**End of transportation
in the 1840s**

# CHANGE AND CONTINUITY: THE LAW-COURTS AND THE BLOODY CODE

Although, as you have seen already in this chapter, this was a period of change, many aspects of the way the law worked remained unchanged:

● You still had to bring the person who had robbed you, or wronged you, to court yourself, and conduct your own case. By the late 19th century the police were beginning to do some of the work of prosecuting criminals. The job of Director of Public Prosecutions began in 1879, but for 30 years could only give advice, not prosecute.

● Lawyers were rarely used in criminal cases. There was still just the accused and the accuser, face to face in court, the way it had been for centuries. Cases were usually over in minutes – a criminal case which lasted an hour was a long one. Juries did not leave the court, but went into a kind of huddle in which most of their arguments could be overheard. It was not unusual for jurymen to fall asleep in the afternoon, following a heavy boozy lunch.

Gradually, in the 19th century, lawyers were used more, at first in very complicated cases. Until 1836 defence lawyers were not allowed to sum up the case for the defence. Only in 1898 was the accused allowed to give evidence on oath. Of course lawyers cost money, so poorer people did not have the option of using them. There was no legal aid (see page 125).

## The end of the Bloody Code

Jeremy Bentham (see also page 71) made some powerful criticisms of the law, some of which are still valid today. He was worried that poor people were excluded from going to court by the expense, the complicated procedures and the use of Latin or old French phrases. He also pointed out that, as we saw on page 51, although there were hundreds of crimes for which you could be hanged – the Bloody Code – they were hardly used, indeed actually avoided. What was the point? he asked. He said it would be better to have fewer hanging offences and greater likelihood of being caught.

Sir Samuel Romilly opposed hanging on the grounds that courts make mistakes and death is the one sentence which cannot be revoked. In 1808 he persuaded Parliament to remove the death penalty for pickpocketing. However, five further attempts to remove the death penalty for stealing items worth 5/- (25p) were all rejected by the House of Lords.

Sir Robert Peel removed the death penalty from 180 separate offences. He also simplified laws, for example, reducing 92 acts concerning theft to one.

Over the 1830s and 1840s the number of offences carrying the death penalty was gradually reduced further. The number of people hanged also fell: in the ten years 1815–1824 an average of 89 were hanged each year, 16 for murder; in 1835–1844 it was 13, with 10 for murder; in 1845–1854 on average nine people were hanged each year, all for murder.

Public hangings were even more rowdy occasions than they had been in the 18th century, see pages 50–51, with lots of crimes committed among the crowd. Many people also felt public hanging was barbaric and it was abolished in 1868.

With hangings greatly reduced and transportation also stopped, prison was now the main punishment for criminals in Britain.

Hanging at Newgate Prison, early 19th century.

# ROOTS OF 19TH-CENTURY PROTEST

## People's grievances

The early years of the Industrial Revolution often brought enormous hardships for ordinary people:

● **At work.** Some craftspeople lost their livelihood because their skills were being replaced by machines; working conditions in factories were long and often unsafe; workers could be laid off at a moment's notice; wages, particularly in farming, were very low (Source 1).

● **At home.** Living conditions in the new cities were unhealthy; the price of food was high.

**SOURCE 1**

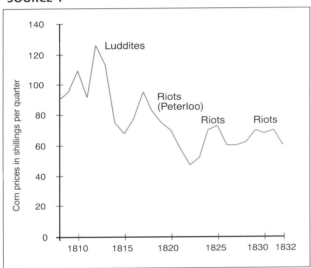

Graph of bread prices and outbreaks of protest in the early 19th century.

## What could they do about these things?

Ordinary people had little power to change things. Only men who owned property, about 4% of the population, had the right to vote. This left working people with only two choices:
(a) To try to persuade the ruling classes to help them, through peaceful petitions, meetings, letters, etc.
(b) Violence: attacks on property, or arson, or riot.

What should be the target of their protests?
Some protests were about work or economic hardship. In this book you can find out about several violent and non-violent versions of this form of protest: the Luddites (page 80), Captain Swing riots (page 81), the Tolpuddle Martyrs (page 110), trade unions (page 111) and the Rebecca Riots (pages 112–13).

Other protests concentrated on trying to change the system of government so that ordinary people had some say in it. They could then pass laws to improve things: see Peterloo (pages 78–79), and the Chartists (pages 82–83).

## Democratic reform

Pressure for a more democratic government in Britain gained strength during the French Revolution, from 1789 onwards. There was great interest in the French revolutionaries, wearing their 'caps of Liberty', calling for 'Liberty, Equality and Fraternity'. Writers, such as Tom Paine, whose *Rights of Man* (1791–92) was on many a cottage bookshelf, and William Cobbett, called for more democracy in Britain.

## Government reaction

The ruling classes were scared stiff. Law and order had not changed from the system described in Chapter 3. It had been set up in the rural Britain of the 17th century. There was no police force, although magistrates could call out the local militia – part-time soldiers – in a crisis. The magistrates, mostly still country landowners, were frightened by the masses of people in the huge new cities, and uncertain how to deal with them.

They certainly did not welcome the French Revolution, but were horrified by it, especially when the French king and aristocrats like themselves were executed by the guillotine (Source 2). Prime Minister William Pitt passed laws to suppress revolutionary ideas: in 1799 the Corresponding Act banned correspondence (letters) with France and in 1799–1800 the Combination Acts banned trade unions.

**SOURCE 2**

The execution of King Louis XVI of France, 1794.

# PROTEST: PETERLOO

From the 1790s to the 1840s there was real fear of revolution in Britain. The worst years were just after 1815, when the wars against Napoleon ended at Waterloo. Factories closed, as they no longer had military contracts; one-third of a million former soldiers and sailors were looking for work; landowners in Parliament passed laws to keep up the price of corn, so bread was expensive.

Many people were desperate. There were huge protest meetings, like the one at Spa Fields, London in 1816, which was addressed by the MP for Preston, Henry Hunt. It was followed by a riot. In 1817 there was a rebellion at Pentrich, in Derbyshire. In 1820 the 'Cato Street conspiracy' was discovered. The conspirators planned to blow up the Cabinet and lead a revolution.

**SOURCE 1**                    An engraving of Peterloo. It was seized by magistrates in Devon in November 1819.

The government responded with harsh repressive measures. Those who pressed for democratic reforms were watched, their letters opened and spies were used to collect information on them. The famous spy 'Oliver' (real name: W. J. Richards) collected evidence to imprison hundreds of people. In 1817, the Prime Minister, Lord Liverpool, suspended 'Habeas Corpus' so that people could be arrested and held without trial. In 1819 the 'Six Acts' gave magistrates powers to search people's houses, put restrictions on holding meetings, banned marching and removed trial by jury.

## Peterloo, 1819

In this atmosphere a large protest meeting was arranged for Monday, 16 August 1819, at St Peter's Fields, Manchester, to call for more democratic representation for Manchester. It was to be addressed by Henry Hunt.

### SOURCE 2

**A** Before 12 o'clock crowds began to assemble, each town or hamlet having a banner, and some a 'Cap of Liberty'. Each party, as it came through the streets, kept in military order, with sticks shouldered . . . It was twenty past one when Hunt appeared: 'Gentlemen, I must ask you to be peaceable; a great deal depends on that, and I trust all who hear me will remain quiet.'

**B** The meeting was addressed by several speakers, showing a menacing attitude . . . The constables were tauntingly insulted . . . About half-past one the magistrates read the Riot Act, and the platform was surrounded. This manoeuvre would have taken place without bloodshed if the mob had not attacked them with missiles. Consequently the cavalry charged in their own defence.

**C** A club of female reformers came from Oldham, and bore a white silk banner inscribed: 'Annual Parliaments, Universal Suffrage and Vote by ballot' . . . 300 to 400 constables marched into the field about 12 o'clock. Not the slightest insult was offered to them. The cavalry drew their swords and brandished them fiercely in the air. Nothing was thrown at them; all was quiet and orderly . . . As soon as Hunt had jumped from the wagon a cry went up from the cavalry 'Have at their flags!' They immediately dashed into the crowd, cutting most indiscriminately to right and left.

*Descriptions of the events at St Peter's Fields, Manchester, 1819 from newspapers.*

What should the magistrates do? Peaceful meetings were legal, but what if it got out of hand? If they feared trouble, magistrates could read the Riot Act; an hour after this they could arrest someone simply for still being there. Should they use this power? What if some of the things Hunt said were treason, or likely to stir up the crowd to riot? Dare they arrest him? How?

The Home Secretary advised them not to react too harshly, but they seem not to have followed his advice. They decided to arrest Hunt, and the militia – untrained cavalry soldiers – went to get him. Violence broke out; at least 11 people were killed and over 400 injured. The event became known as Peterloo, a sarcastic reference to the battle of Waterloo.

1. Use your own knowledge to explain why the magistrates would find the description of the crowd in Source 2A worrying or frightening.
2. How does Source 2B try to defend the actions of: the magistrates? the militia?
3. Use Sources 2A and 2C and your own knowledge to explain what the protesters wanted and how they were going to achieve these things.
4. In what ways does Source 2B disagree with Source 2C?
5. How does Source 1 help you understand the events at Peterloo better?
6. Source 1 is an artist's drawing. How does this affect how you use this source?
7. Use all of Source 2 to comment on the accuracy of Source 1.
8. Source 1 was taken from a man in Devon, in November. What does this tell you about national reactions to Peterloo?
9. The owner of this picture (Source 1) was arrested for having it on him. Why do you think the magistrates did this?
10. Which of the extracts in Source 2 supports the interpretation of Peterloo given in Source 1?
11. Use these sources and your own knowledge to explain what you think happened at Peterloo.

# PROTEST: LUDDITES AND CAPTAIN SWING

## KEY QUESTION
◆ *How can technological change lead to violent protest?*

As we saw on page 59, one of the factors bringing about the Industrial Revolution in Britain was new technology. But changes in technology did not come without painful consequences for some people. We are going to look at two case-studies of protest, one industrial, one rural, to see how this happened.

## The Luddites

Life for many industrial workers was hard in the early 19th century, as we have seen. In the textile industry, machines had taken over many jobs. However some tasks, such as weaving, or shearing, still needed skilled workers who could therefore earn good money. From 1811 to 1816 new machines were set up which threatened the livelihoods of these workers: large knitting-frames in the stocking-weaving areas of Derbyshire, Nottinghamshire and Leicestershire, shearing-frames in west Yorkshire and weaving looms in Lancashire.

The proud skilled workers faced ruin, but what could they do? They could not vote; trade unions were banned (see page 77); the magistrates and the government supported the factory-owners. In their fear and anger and powerlessness they wanted to smash the machines, but they knew that the punishments for attacking property were fierce.

### SOURCE 1

They broke only the frames of such as have reduced men's wages. In one house last night they broke four frames out of six. The other two belonged to masters who had not lowered wages and were not touched.

*Report of Luddite actions in the newspaper* The Leeds Mercury, *1812.*

### SOURCE 2

Sir, Information has just been given that you are a holder of those detestable shearing-frames and I was asked by my men to write to you to give you fair warning to pull them down. If they are not taken down by the end of the week, I shall send at least 300 men to destroy them.

Signed, NED LUDD

*A letter from 'Ned Ludd'.*

They therefore took extreme care to protect their identities: they invented secret ways of communicating (Source 3) and claimed to follow a made-up leader, 'Ned Ludd'.

### SOURCE 3

You must raise your right hand over your right eye – if there be another Luddite in the company he will raise his left hand over his left eye – then you must raise the forefinger of your right hand to the right side of your mouth – the other will raise the little finger of his left hand to the left side of his mouth and will say What are you? The answer: Determined. He will say What for? Your answer: Free liberty. Then he will converse with you and tell you anything he knows.

*An informer describes how Luddites tried to keep their actions secret, 1812.*

The government portrayed them as mindless vandals and thugs, but they carried out their attacks on machines quite carefully. Source 1 describes how they avoided those machines belonging to employers who treated them fairly. Once they had started machine-smashing, they could use threats to get what they wanted (Source 2). One historian, E. J. Hobsbawm, has called this kind of action 'collective bargaining by riot.'

The situation soon became serious. A factory in Lancashire was burned down. Two Luddites died in an attack on Rawfolds Mill, near Huddersfield and a factory-owner was murdered in Yorkshire. By late 1812 12,000 troops were stationed in west Yorkshire and government spies were everywhere. Despite their precautions, Luddites were arrested. In Lancashire four were hanged and 17 transported; in Yorkshire 14 were hanged and in the north Midlands 1,000 were fined and seven transported. Nowhere were the new machines withdrawn.

## 'Captain Swing'

Although we hear more about industrial workers and conditions in towns, farmworkers were definitely worse off at this time. Their wages were lower than in industry and they could be laid off, unpaid, if there was no work to do on the farm. Their housing was also worse, and they were expected to defer at all times to the farmer who employed them. As with the Luddites, there was also a general feeling of resentment at Britain's undemocratic and oppressive government.

Hayricks set on fire by 'Captain Swing' rioters.

## Threshing-machines

One job which kept labourers employed in the winter was threshing, by hand, using a flail. The invention of the threshing-machine threatened to rob them even of this work.

Furthermore, harvests in 1828 and 1829 were bad. This meant high food prices. It also meant that farmers were worse off and tried to cut wages.

The farmworkers were just as powerless as the Luddites. In the autumn of 1830 there were outbreaks of violence all over southern and eastern England. Hayricks were burned and threshing-machines smashed (Source 4). It was an enormous rising: 20 counties were seriously affected. Between January 1830 and September 1832 there were 316 cases of arson and 390 attacks on threshing-machines. The protesters used a made-up leader for themselves, in this case 'Captain Swing', and threatening letters were sent in his name.

Just as with the Luddites, the authorities cracked down hard: 19 people were hanged, including a 12-year-old boy, 581 were transported and 644 jailed. Despite this, there is some evidence that farmers were pushed into keeping wages up: insurance companies wanted to know their reputation among the labourers before granting them fire insurance. Probably, also, the widespread introduction of threshing-machines was held up for 30 years or so.

❖ *Take two sheets of paper. Divide each of them into four. Head the sections: long-term causes; the machines; violent protest; results. Write one sentence under each section for each of the protests.*
❖ *What similarities and differences can you see?*
❖ *Most of the middle and upper classes thought of industrial workers as stupid, uneducated, prone to acts of mindless violence.*
*(i) How far does the information here support that interpretation? Make a list of points.*
*(ii) How far does the information here contradict that interpretation? Make another list. Expand your list into a paragraph of continuous writing.*

# PROTEST: THE CHARTISTS

## KEY QUESTION
◆ *Did the Chartists adopt the right tactics?*

Chartism was the biggest popular protest movement of the 19th century. Between 1836 and 1848, millions of people took part in demonstrations, marches and collecting signatures for three giant petitions. These asked Parliament to adopt the six points of the Charter to make Britain more democratic:

1. The vote for all adult males.
2. Secret ballot (so that your employer or anyone else could not influence how you voted).
3. Annual elections to Parliament.
4. No property qualification for MPs (so that working people could stand for Parliament).
5. Payment of MPs (also to help working people become MPs).
6. Equal-sized constituencies.

◆ *Why did working-class people support Chartism?*

● The grievances of working-class people over working and living conditions, described on page 77, were as bad as ever.

● The 1832 Reform Act disappointed many people who wanted a more democratic Britain. Popular protests had helped to get it passed, but the number of people allowed to vote was only doubled, to 8% of all males.

● The Grand National Consolidated Trade Union (see page 85) collapsed in 1835. Those who had high hopes that trade unions would solve working people's problems now turned to Chartism.

● There were other motives, including opposition to Peel's new police force, 1829, and the new Poor Law, 1834.

For a while millions of people saw the Charter as the answer to all their problems. The first petition, containing 1.3 million signatures, was submitted in 1839. Parliament rejected it. The Chartists now faced the problem facing other pressure groups such as the suffragettes (see page 100): how do you win over an unwilling Parliament?

There seemed to be four possible courses of action:

**(a) Moral force**, which Lovett supported (Source 1). However, it was hard to persuade desperate, hungry supporters to follow this line when it had failed once.

## SOURCE 1

Let us, friends, unite together the honest, moral, hard-working and thinking members of society. Let us publish our views so that we create a moral, thinking energetic force in politics.

*Chartist leader William Lovett, 1838.*

**(b) Industrial action:** a month-long strike of all workers, a general strike or 'national holiday'. The trouble with this plan was that most supporters could not afford to stay off work for a month.

**(c) Violence: an armed uprising.** Some Chartists, such as George Julian Harney (Source 2), supported this. Over the next few years there were several outbreaks of Chartist violence, of which the most spectacular was the rising by Welsh Chartists at Newport in 1839, in which 14 people were killed. Many Chartists expected a revolution would come sooner or later and some were armed (Source 3).

## SOURCE 2

Universal suffrage there will be – or our tyrants will find to their cost that we will make of our country one vast howling wilderness of desolation and destruction. Believe me, there is no argument like the sword, and the musket is unanswerable.

*George Julian Harney, in the Chartist newspaper* Northern Star *in 1839.*

## SOURCE 3

I bought a gun, although I knew it was a serious thing for a Chartist to have a gun in his possession. It might be said that we were fools, but young people now have no idea what we had to endure. From 1842 to 1848 I earned less than 9s (45p) a week.

*Benjamin Wilson, an old Chartist, writing in 1887.*

**(d) The threat of violence: physical force.** 'Peacefully if we can, forcibly if we must' was the line taken by the new leader of the movement, Feargus O'Connor.

In 1839 the Chartists held a Convention in London, with 53 representatives from all over the country, paid for by their local groups. Some have argued that this was the first democratic Parliament in Britain. They decided to support physical force. The trouble was that it was impossible to separate out those who only

## SOURCE 5

Police ready for action at the time of the Third Chartist petition, 1848.

threatened violence from those who actually wanted a revolution. The government realised that O'Connor was bluffing, but the physical force policy turned most middle- and upper-class people against the Chartists.

A second petition was presented, and rejected, in 1842. This was followed by a wave of strikes in the north of England. This year saw Britain close to a revolution, with widespread violent protests and hundreds of arrests. However, the government had soldiers ready. General Napier, their commander, recognised the real distress which provided the root-cause of Chartism, but was well-organised against them (Source 4).

## SOURCE 4

(i) 1839: 'The streets of this town are horrible. The poor starving people go about begging.'

(ii) 1842: 'Poor people! They have set all England against them and their physical force. Fools! We have the physical force, not they. They talk of a hundred thousand men. Who is to move them when I am dancing around them with cavalry and pelting them with cannon-shot?'

*From the diary of Sir Charles Napier, commander of government forces in the north of England.*

The terrible poverty of 1847 and 1848 led to the last Chartist agitation. Again there were angry speeches and massive demonstrations. A third petition was prepared in 1848, said to contain over 5 million signatures. A mass meeting was held at Kennington, south London. The government was worried – there had been a revolution in France in 1848 – but acted much more effectively than the magistrates at Peterloo in 1819. 150,000 special constables were taken on; 7,000 troops were ready, and more were waiting near railway stations (Source 5). They controlled all the railway and telegraph systems. The bridges across the Thames were guarded. O'Connor was told that the Chartists could not march to Parliament; he agreed to deliver the petition by cab. The Chartists went home peacefully. The petition was found to have only 2 million signatures and was rejected again. Some Chartists, notably William Cuffay, the black Chartist, would have risen but the leaders realised it was hopeless.

Chartism may have failed utterly at the time, but British working people had learnt how to organise themselves, to run newspapers, meetings and be heard. Over the next 50 years all but one of the six points of the Charter became law.

❖ *Divide into four groups. You are all delegates at the 1839 Chartist Convention. Look at the four possible courses of action the Chartists could take. In each case:*
  *– describe what you think the Chartists should do (use quotations from the sources to help you where possible);*
  *– explain why your policy would be successful;*
  *– explain why the other three would be bound to fail.*

# PROTEST: TRADE UNIONS AND THE 1889 DOCK STRIKE

*KEY QUESTION*

◆ *Why did it take so long for trade unions for unskilled workers to get started?*

## Early unions

There were unions of skilled workers before the Industrial Revolution, called 'trade societies'. Members paid a subscription and received benefits such as help in sickness or old age. During the 1790s, when the government was frightened of all kinds of working-class activity, it passed the Combination Acts, 1799 and 1800, to ban them. In fact, these acts did not really stop trade unions, but made it even harder to get one going. Those who joined a union were simply sacked. Unskilled factory workers, living on the breadline, could not afford to pay a union subscription.

The Combination Acts were repealed in 1824 and unions began to grow in some areas (Source 1).

**SOURCE 1**
Membership card of the Women's Trade union, 1833.

**SOURCE 2**

The object of this society is to raise funds for the support of its members in case of sickness, accident, old age, for the burial of members and their wives, emigration, loss of tools by fire, water or theft and for assistance to members out of work.

*Robert Applegarth, Secretary of the Amalgamated Society of Carpenters (a 'New Model Union'), speaking in 1867.*

**SOURCE 3**
London docks in the late 19th century.

Robert Owen tried to form a union of all workers: The Grand National Consolidated Trade Union. In 1834 he had 1/2 million members. However, he found it hard to hold it all together, particularly after the Tolpuddle Martyrs Case in 1834 (see page 111), and it collapsed.

For the next 30 years most working-class effort went into Chartism (see pages 82–83). Then, in the 1860s, came the 'New Model Unions.' These were for skilled workers, paying a high (1/- = 5p) subscription. This paid for a national organisation, with officials who used the new penny post and railway system to keep members in touch. They paid good benefits (Source 2), including strike pay. If it came to a strike, employers were hit hard as these skilled workers were crucial to a business and could not be as easily replaced by 'blackleg' labour as unskilled workers could.

## SOURCE 4

Then begins the scuffling and scrambling forth of countless hands high in the air to catch the eye of him whose voice may give them work. As the foreman calls from a book of names, some men jump upon the backs of others so as to attract the notice of him who hires them. All are shouting, some cry aloud his surname, some his Christian name. Now the appeal is made in Irish, now in broken English. Indeed it is a sight to sadden the most callous, to see thousands of men struggling for one day's hire.

*In 1860 Henry Mayhew described dockers waiting to be called for work.*

## SOURCE 5

The poor fellows are miserably clad, with scarcely a boot on their feet. There are men who come to work in our dock without a bit of food in their stomachs; they work for an hour and earn 5d (2p). Their hunger will not allow them to continue; by 4 o'clock their strength is utterly gone.

*A dock owner describes the dockers' situation in the 1880s.*

## SOURCE 6

Tens of thousands of tons of food was rotting in the ships lying in the Thames, which was over-crowded with vessels which could neither unload their cargo nor go elsewhere. It is satisfactory to have it proved that workers have the destiny of the world in their own hands.

*The newspaper* Reynolds News *describes the effects of the strike, 1 September 1889.*

Unions for unskilled workers, however, still did not exist and only about 5% of all workers were in a trade union. Attempts in the 1870s to set up a National Agricultural Labourers' Union, for example, failed. Then, in the late 1880s, there were successful strikes of the match-girls (1888), and the gas workers (1889). In the same year came the London Dock Strike.

### The 1889 Dock Strike

Unloading ships at the busy London docks (Source 3) was almost entirely done by hand. There were skilled workers, with their own unions, but most of the dockers were hired by the hour, in a humiliating system called 'the cage' (Sources 4 and 5). The foreman chose who should work from a clamouring mass of dockers. Wages were 5d (2p) an hour.

Ben Tillett was secretary of a small union of tea-warehousemen who began a strike for a pay increase to 6d (2.5p) an hour: the 'docker's tanner' (tanner was slang for sixpence). Soon, encouraged by other strikes of unskilled men such as the gas workers, other dockers joined in. Other organisers, socialists like John Burns and Tom Mann, helped to bring London docks to a standstill. A huge procession wound its way through London, ending in a huge meeting in Hyde Park.

The strike organisers were successful in winning public sympathy for the dockers. Lots of people gave money for the strikers, but after two weeks their funds were nearly dry and it looked as if they would be forced back to work. Then £30,000 arrived from trade unionists in Australia. The port owners were put under pressure as the strike meant ships were lying idle in the river, with their cargoes rotting and valueless (Source 6). After five weeks Cardinal Manning helped to end the strike and the 'docker's tanner' was won.

❖ *Why was it hard to get unions for unskilled workers going?*
*Read the text and make a list of all the points you can find. Group these under: the law; employers' attitudes; workers' attitudes; organisation problems. Write four paragraphs, using your list and these sections.*

❖ *What part did the following play in the success of the 1889 Dock Strike:*
*public sympathy; organisation; the dockers' desperation; Australian money; the dockers' solidarity?*
*In each case, explain how the item contributed to the success of the strike.*

# THE STORY 5
# 20TH-CENTURY BRITAIN

| 1900 | | |
|---|---|---|
| | 1901 | National fingerprint record started |
| | 1902 | Schools for offenders aged 15–21 started at Borstal |
| | 1903 | WSPU (suffragettes) formed |
| | 1907 | Probation Service starts |
| | 1908 | Children's Act: separate treatment of children at law |
| 1910 | 1910 | Arrest of the murderer Dr Crippen, using radio |
| | 1914 | Outbreak of First World War |
| | 1918 | Votes for some women: women can become JPs |
| 1920 | 1920 | Women allowed to join police |
| | 1926 | General Strike |
| | 1928 | Votes for all women |
| 1930 | | |
| | 1932 | Approved schools for offenders under 15 |
| | 1933 | Worst year of Depression: 3 million unemployed |
| | 1936 | First open prison at Wakefield Jail |
| 1940 | 1939 | Outbreak of Second World War |
| | 1948 | Attendance centres started |
| 1950 | | |
| 1960 | | |
| | 1965 | Abolition of death penalty; Race Relations Act |
| 1970 | | |
| | 1971 | Crown Courts set up |
| | 1975 | Sex Discrimination Act |
| 1980 | 1981 | Riots in Brixton |
| | 1982 | Borstals abolished |
| | 1984 | IRA Brighton bomb |
| | 1985 | Football riot at Heysel Stadium |
| 1990 | 1990 | Riot at Strangeways Jail, Manchester |
| 2000 | | |

## Standard of living

The prosperity of Britain in the late 19th century continued up to the First World War (1914–1918). The cost of this war, and the Second World War (1939–1945) toppled Britain from her dominant position in world trade. However, from the late 1950s most people's standard of living improved greatly.

## Divisions

The rise in living standards was not evenly shared. In the Depression of the 1930s, half of Britain suffered severe unemployment. Unemployment returned in the 1980s and in the 1990s millions remained out of work. The gap between rich and poor increased in the last part of the 20th century.

## Welfare State

Begun by the Liberals before the First World War, developed by Labour after the Second World War, a welfare state was set up. This meant that the government tried to remove the threat of poverty or ill-health from all citizens, to provide security 'from the cradle to the grave'.

## Technology

New technology has utterly changed people's lives. Car ownership and air travel have brought mobility and freedom. First cinema and radio, then TV, have transformed entertainment. Computers have revolutionised work.

# CRIME IN THE 20TH CENTURY

## KEY QUESTIONS

◆ *How has the pattern of crime changed during this century?*

◆ *How does poverty affect crime?*

◆ *What do crime statistics mean?*

Crime figures for the years since 1860 show a 'J'-shaped curve (Source 1).

## 1. 1860–1955

Crime fell by 43% between 1860 and 1900. It was then static and low until about 1930, followed by a slight rise. Several reasons are put forward for this:

● Britain was more prosperous than it had been before, at least until 1930, and this prosperity was more widely spread.

● There was more democracy and trade union growth, so less dissatisfaction.

● The new police had won acceptance and respect. People took pride in the fact that they were unarmed and genuinely believed that 'the British bobby was the best in the world'. People felt that the streets were safer than they had been in the 1850s.

● Certain petty crimes had declined: drunkenness was responsible for 25% of all offences in the 1870s but by the 20th century it had declined as there were more alternatives to the pub. Tramps, beggars and street-traders disappeared from the streets, partly as a result of determined police action, partly with changing habits and partly because sleeping rough was no longer defined as a crime after 1935.

## SOURCE 1

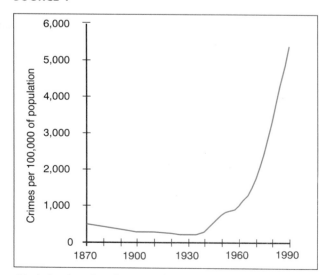

Graph showing crimes known to the police, 1860–1980. To take into account rising population, the figures are shown per 100,000 people.

**Crime and the 1930s Depression.** Unemployment in Britain in 1933 reached 3 million – about 22% of all workers. In some old industrial areas of north-east England, south Wales and central Scotland nearly everyone was out of work for most of the 1930s. The dole gave them enough to live on – just. But people were desperately poor. How did this affect crime?

In the past, the link between poverty and crime had been very clear. There was an increase in crime at times of high food prices. There was even a link between cold weather and more crime, as people stole fuel or items to sell to buy fuel. Did the poverty caused by unemployment turn people like the man in Source 2 to crime?

Source 1 shows some increase in crime after 1930, but this may be simply the growth of motoring offences as car ownership in more prosperous areas of Britain became more common. In fact there was no real increase in crime in hard-hit areas (Source 3). Why not?

## SOURCE 2

Unemployed man, 1930s. Why didn't this man turn to crime?

## SOURCE 3

One of the most remarkable features of the Depression has been the absence of serious crime among unemployed workers.

*The writer George Orwell comments on crime in depressed areas in the 1930s.*

Nick Leeson, whose illegal speculation led to the collapse of Barings Bank in 1995.

The answer is that those who turn to crime at times of poverty are not the type of people hit by unemployment in the 1930s. Crime is mainly committed by young people, particularly those in casual jobs, soon laid off in difficult times. Middle-aged, skilled workers, family men like the man in Source 2, having been law-abiding all their lives, are not suddenly going to turn to theft.

## 2. 1955 to the present day

As Source 1 shows, there has been an enormous increase in crime since 1955. The number of reported crimes doubled in the 1960s, and is now 20 times the figure for 1955. In 1960 there were 0.75 million serious offences known to the police; in 1992 there were 5.6 million. Nine-tenths of all offences in this period were crimes against property, but crimes against the person have increased just as dramatically. In 1945 there were 5,000 cases of violence against the person recorded by the police; by 1960 the figure had risen to 16,000 and by the early 1990s to over 200,000.

Most of the people who committed these crimes were young men (only one female appears in court for every seven males). Two-thirds of crimes are committed by males under 25, half by young men under 20. The age-group for boys with the highest proportion of offenders is 15–16, (14–15 for girls).

As these years since 1955 have been years of the greatest prosperity in British history, we have to look to causes other than poverty.

## Problems with crime statistics

Since the 19th century we have had many more statistics for crime and criminals. But what do they actually tell us?

**(a) Reporting the crime.** Research shows that large numbers of crimes are never reported to the police: only 22% of acts of vandalism and 18% of thefts from a house, for example, are reported. There are many reasons for this: people may be embarrassed, afraid of reprisals, or do not want to get involved in a private dispute. The offence may be too petty, or involve members of the family.

In some areas, people mistrust the police, so do not report crimes. The Merseyside Crime Survey, 1984, found that 21% of people in a working-class district had witnessed a car theft, but only 4% in a suburban area. Yet the actual figures for reported car theft were almost the same for both areas.

**(b) Recording the crime.** The police make their own judgements about whether or not to record a crime. The figures thus reflect their decisions.

**(c) Changes in attitudes of public and police.** The most striking example of this is the rise in number of reported and recorded cases of family violence and sexual assault. In both cases, there were strong pressures in the past not to report these crimes and on police not to record them. In recent years women have been encouraged not to hide these offences and police have been pressed to take them more seriously. Are the numbers of these crimes really increasing, or are more being reported and recorded?

**(d) White-collar crime.** Some people argue that we focus too much on working-class crime and street crime and ignore 'white-collar' crime. This can vary from using your employer's pens, paper, phone or computer to fiddling your expenses. Waiters may fiddle the bills, garages may not do the work you have paid for and employers break safety regulations. Very little of this type of crime is reported. Business fraud in the City of London is estimated at £1 billion a year, yet the City prefers to be self-regulating and the police may not have the financial expertise to investigate these highly complicated crimes (Source 4).

❖ *What do you think are the causes of the 'crime wave' which has overcome Britain since the late 1950s?*

❖ *Why don't people record crimes? Ask questions of your family and adult friends; compare answers across the class.*

❖ *Is 'white-collar' crime as serious as street crime?*

# NEW CRIMES: CRIMES AGAINST PROPERTY

*KEY QUESTION*
◆ *What is new about 20th-century crime?*
◆ *How has modern technology changed crime?*
◆ *Why has car crime become so important?*

## Motor car crime

The first motor cars appeared on British roads in 1894; by 1939 60% of all the cases coming before magistrates, and a quarter of all crime, involved motor cars. Why? There is more to it than the kinds of crimes which involved horses and carts in the 19th century now being applied to motor cars. As you read this, look for as many differences as you can.

**1. Car ownership.** Owners have to meet several legal requirements before they can even start the engine. They have to have insurance, tax, driving licence (having passed a test), the car has to be roadworthy, (and MOT tested if it is over three years old). Once on the road, drivers have to drive according to all the laws of the road (signs and speed limits, etc.) with care and attention, not under the influence of drugs or alcohol (Source 2). All these laws are necessary because motor accidents can kill people. By 1939, 6,500 people a year were being killed, with only 2 million cars on the roads. (Today, with 22 million cars, the figure is just over 4,000).

Enforcing all these regulations meant lots of new work for the police. Until the invention of traffic lights, many of them spent long tedious hours on point duty at road junctions. Road traffic offences brought the police up against the middle classes, who made up most of the car owners. Before then, four-fifths of all crime had involved working-class offenders.

### SOURCE 1

Across the centuries, no form of activity has had so profound an effect on relations between the law and the public in so short a time.

*Textbook authors, 1996, commenting on the impact of the car.*

**2. Car crime: theft.** About half of all thefts involve stealing cars or stealing goods from cars. Stolen cars are usually altered to give them a new identity. Crooked car-dealers turn back the mileometer on second-hand cars in order to get better prices for them. In this they are not that different from the crooked horse-traders of previous centuries, who were expert at changing the look of a horse. Sometimes cars are stolen to be used in another crime, such as robbery. Car radios, stereos and personal belongings are stolen for profit.

### SOURCE 2

Police enforcing the law about drinking and driving.

**3. Car crime: joyriding.** This means stealing a car and using it to ride around before abandoning or crashing it (Source 3). It is done by young people, sometimes as young as ten. The motive is simply excitement, but, even apart from the loss of property, people can be killed.

### SOURCE 3
Joyrider spinning a stolen car on a wet road at night.

## Shoplifting

The amount of shoplifting has doubled each decade since the 1950s. An important factor in this is the change in the way we do our shopping, from small shops and market stalls to huge supermarkets and shopping centres. Seeing large amounts of desirable goods on display seems to be too much of a temptation for many people. Shoplifters fall into various groups: some are simply very poor, some are mentally ill, some are alcoholics, some are young people looking for excitement. Strangely, many shoplifters actually have enough money on them to pay for the goods they have stolen.

## Smuggling

In the 20th century better transport has made smuggling harder to stop. With so many millions of people travelling in and out of the country, by land, sea and air, including by private aeroplane, the task is enormous.

As in the past, anything which is restricted in its movement into the country becomes a smuggle-able item, see page 54. After 1945 imported watches had to pay a duty of 33%, so smugglers brought them in by the hundreds. They used special overcoats, secret compartments in cars, etc. As soon as the duty was removed the trade stopped.

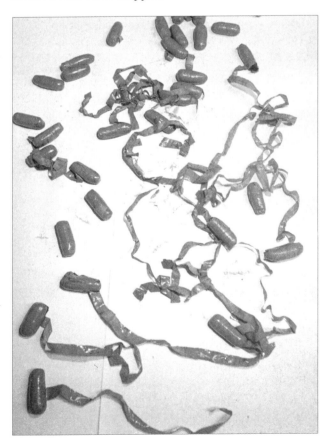

Today there is smuggling of immigrants, who would otherwise not be let into Britain. But most common, and most difficult to stop, is drug-smuggling. Demand for illegal drugs has increased in the last 30 years. They are easy to smuggle, as small quantities are worth a great deal. Customs officers wage a continuing war against well-organised, international drug-dealers (Source 4).

## Computer crime

The introduction and widespread use of computers has led to all kinds of crimes, some new, some just new versions of old crimes.

There is stealing computer time, either by using someone else's computer for your own business, or using someone else's password so that they are charged, not you. There is diverting money from other people's accounts to your own or getting the system to make out cheques to you. There is breaking into other companies' confidential information, which can be sold to a competitor. There is computer vandalism, often done by disgruntled employees: using a powerful magnet to destroy files, or installing a virus so that the system crashes.

The people who carry out these crimes are usually individuals, some of them extremely talented. Committing the crime is seen as a challenge. Because computers are new, and changing fast, it is hard for the forces of law and order to keep up with, and catch the criminals. Financial institutions, like banks, who have gone over to computerisation in a big way have had to work out new security procedures.

❖ *List the ways new technology has affected crimes against property.*
❖ *Which of the crimes described here are new crimes and which are old crimes in a new form?*
❖ *Use the information here and your knowledge to say how far you agree or disagree with the opinion of the authors in Source 1.*

**SOURCE 4**
Illegal drugs taken from the stomach of an air passenger who had tried to smuggle drugs into the country.

# CRIME IN THE 20TH CENTURY: CRIMES AGAINST THE PERSON

*KEY QUESTION*
◆ *How have crimes against the person changed in the last 50 years?*

## Murder

The most controversial thing to happen this century to the crime of murder was the abolition of the death penalty in 1965. As with any change in the law, it was passed by Parliament. A majority of public opinion wants to bring back the death penalty and MPs have discussed it again many times since. Each time those in favour of bringing back hanging have lost the vote. The sentence for murder is now prison for 'life'. In some cases this may mean that the murderer will be let out after ten years. But in more serious or horrific cases – murder of a police officer, or murder in the course of a robbery, or terrorism, or murder of children – it will mean prison for at least 20 years, even the rest of the murderer's life.

The number of murders in Britain has risen slowly over the years, and was in fact rising before hanging was abolished. In 1957 there were 429 murders; in 1995 there were 906. However, this rise is less than the rise in all other types of crime described on page 89.

We hear a great deal about the most horrific murders: multiple murders, or murders of children, or murders involving sex. However, most murders are not like this: in 75% of murders, the victim was well-known to the murderer, who had never committed any other crime.

## Terrorism

Many people have strong beliefs: they want a change in society or in the law. As we have seen in this book, there are many ways of going about getting things changed. Terrorists believe that they can only get what they want by acts of violence against property or people. For example, quite a number of people oppose the use of animals in laboratory experiments; a few of them, belonging to the Animal Liberation Front, have committed acts of violence by blowing up cars or buildings belonging to those who work in such laboratories.

The IRA, the Irish Republican Army, believe that British rule in Northern Ireland should be ended. Since the 1970s they have used violence against the ruling Protestant majority in Northern Ireland. In return, Protestant terrorist groups, such as the Ulster Defence Association (UDA), have been set up.

**SOURCE 1**

Scene after an IRA bombing in Bishopsgate, London, in April 1993.

At times the IRA have carried out murders or attacks on buildings on the British mainland. They say that they do this to point out to the British people that their grievance still exists and won't go away. In 1984 they tried to blow up the entire British Cabinet at the Grand Hotel in Brighton; they have launched mortar shells at 10 Downing Street. They have also exploded bombs in pubs, railway stations, office blocks and shopping centres (Source 1). Ordinary members of the public have been killed: for example, a bomb at Warrington in 1993 killed two small boys.

This has led to a number of results:

● The Police Special Branch spend their time trying to catch terrorists, if possible before they plant bombs.

● Terrorists who are caught and found guilty receive very long prison sentences: 30 or 40 years.

● The police have to take special precautions to try to protect the public. This may mean closing down railway or tube stations if there is a danger of a bomb, causing huge disruption to people's lives. They have to balance the safety of the public against making security so tight that normal life becomes impossible.

**SOURCE 2**

Rioters confront police in the streets of Brixton, south London, 1981.

**SOURCE 3**

*Lord Scarman headed an enquiry into the Brixton riots of 1981. In his report he said:*

Racial disadvantage is a fact of current British life. It was, I am sure, a significant factor in the Brixton disorders . . .

The police must carry some responsibility . . . The community and community leaders must take their share of the blame for distrust and mutual suspicion between the community and the police.

## Racial violence

In the early 20th century, there were occasional outbreaks of violence against immigrant communities: for example, Chinese seamen in Cardiff in 1911, or Jews in East London in the 1930s. Since then the victims have almost always been black people. In 1958 and 1962, black people's homes in London were attacked. From the 1980s there have been racial attacks on Asians and Caribbeans on the streets and in their homes, particularly in the east end of London. People have been killed in stabbings and arson attacks. Sometimes these attacks have been incited by right-wing political groups.

After 1975 another element entered the picture: riots by young black people against the police. This started with anti-police violence following the Notting Hill carnivals of 1976 and 1977. More serious riots occurred in Bristol in 1980 and Brixton (London) in 1981 (Source 2). These last riots were soon followed by riots in Toxteth (Liverpool), Moss Side (Manchester) and Handsworth (Birmingham) in the same year. More riots took place through the 1980s.

Usually the spark which set off the riot was an attempt by the police to arrest someone. Certainly relations between police and the local black communities were bad. Researchers have pointed out that the Brixton riot came just after a police operation called 'Swamp 81', in which over 1,000 people were stopped and searched. Only 100 people were charged, most of these only with offences, like obstruction, which would not have occurred if the police had not stopped them.

The judgement of Lord Scarman on the causes of the Brixton riot is given in Source 3. The first of his list of causes, what he called 'racial disadvantage', means continued racist prejudice leading to high black unemployment and poor housing.

Since the 1980s all kinds of efforts have been made to deal with the roots of these riots, not least by the police themselves. But the big underlying problems of inner-city life, like bad housing and racist attitudes in the job market, still remain.

❖ *Whether or not Britain should have the death penalty for murder remains a controversial issue. Before discussing it, collect some more information: (i) Think about the different purposes of punishment given on page 7. Which should be most important in murder cases? (ii) What does history tell us about this issue? (iii) What do other countries do? Find out about European countries, the USA, Australia. What do they do? What is the result?*

# CRIME AND YOUNG PEOPLE IN THE 20TH CENTURY

*KEY QUESTIONS*

◆ *Is the age we live in more violent than other periods in history?*
◆ *How do young people get involved in violence?*

## A violent age?

Some people claim that we are living in a violent age. They point to the things already mentioned in this chapter – a rise in violent crime, riots, terrorism – and the topics discussed here (hooliganism and vandalism). But is this age more violent than any in the past? More violent than the medieval period, for example, when gangs of armed retainers roamed the country with no-one to stop them (see Chapter 2)? More violent than the Early Modern period, with public hangings and highwaymen on the roads (see Chapter 3)? More violent than the industrial age, when criminals flourished in a country almost without police (see Chapter 4)?

How would you measure whether we are living in a more violent age than any in the past?

What statistics would you want? Are people's impressions more, or less, important than statistics?

## Young people and violence

The division often made between crimes against the person and crimes against property has little meaning here. In certain situations gangs of young people, almost always boys, become violent; the objects of their violence might be property or another person.

In the 1960s gang rivalry focused around 'Mods', who rode motor-scooters (Source 1), and 'Rockers', who rode motorbikes. They also adopted different styles of clothes and tastes in music, although there was little else to distinguish between them. In the late 1960s 'skinheads' appeared. They liked to appear 'hard', were often racist, and linked their search for violence to football.

**SOURCE 1**

'Mods' at Brighton, 1964.

### SOURCE 2

In 1888 a referee complained that the crowd at Bolton were 'dirty-nosed little rascals who spoil every football match they go to'.

A newspaper reported he had been attacked by 'a hail of empty bottles'.

## Football hooligans

'Hooliganism' is not new: the name comes from an unruly group of Irish workers in south-east London in the late 19th century. Nor is the link with football new: violent fans went 'on the rampage', as the newspapers like to describe it, in the late 19th century. Matches were abandoned and referees had to hide from angry crowds, see Source 2.

This kind of behaviour disappeared between the wars, only to emerge again around 1960. Gangs of rival supporters, often drunk, fought each other, inflicting serious injuries, even, occasionally, death. If a fight did not take place, gangs would attack houses, cars, pubs, shops, railway trains and so on. Some gangs of supporters were well-organised, with middle-class leaders, who planned how to outwit police attempts to contain them. The most notorious incident was in 1985, at the Heysel Stadium in Belgium, when gangs of British fans attacked Italian fans. In the panic a wall collapsed and 38 people were killed.

By the 1990s uncontrolled football hooliganism on a grand scale was rare, for two main reasons:

**(a)** The police developed tactics for keeping rival groups of supporters apart. They are escorted from the moment they arrive in town until their departure. Particularly troublesome offenders were sentenced to Attendance Centres (see page 109), which they had to go to on Saturday afternoons, so missing football matches.

**(b)** Football grounds have changed, with much more seating and separate secure areas for different supporters.

**SOURCE 3**

Football hooligans confront riot police.

**SOURCE 4**

Graffiti in a subway.

## Vandalism

This term covers a wide range of actions. Here are some examples:
**a** damaging car tyres,
**b** writing on a wall with an aerosol paint spray (Source 4),
**c** dropping heavy items from a tower block,
**d** smashing up telephone boxes,
**e** breaking a street light bulb,
**f** carving your name on a desk at school,
**g** tearing up flowers or trees in a park or garden,
**h** breaking a car radio aerial,
**i** breaking a shop window,
**j** putting large objects on to a railway line.

1. Put these acts of vandalism in order of seriousness.
2. Do you regard any, or all of them as crimes?
3. What punishments would you give for each of these?

Acts of vandalism like those listed above are nearly always carried out by young people. They are the sorts of crimes that seem to make older people very angry, more angry than more 'serious' crimes, such as robbery. This may be because the objects damaged are used, or admired, or needed daily by other people. It also annoys people that the sentences vandals receive if they are caught are light: after all, the cost of the damage caused may not be very much. Some people have suggested that the 'shaming punishments' (see page 38) would be more suitable for this kind of crime.

❖ *What do you think are the causes of vandalism?*
❖ *What suggestions do you have for stopping vandalism?*
❖ *What punishments do you think vandals should receive?*

# ATTITUDES TO CRIME TODAY

## The press and television

Crime is news (it always has been, see Source 6 on page 62). Both newspapers and TV are keen to sell more papers or attract more viewers by telling a good story. This may mean paying more attention to certain types of crime than to others. In the 1980s the press began to write about a 'new' sort of crime, called mugging. Black youngsters were usually blamed. In fact, it is doubtful that the crime was 'new', whether street crime was increasing and whether black youths were more likely to commit this sort of crime than white youths.

One result of media attention on crime is to obscure the fact that, although there is a lot of crime in inner cities, many suburban and rural areas suffer little more crime than 30 years ago. Also, the sums involved are often small: in 1996, a quarter of all break-ins led to nothing of value being stolen, and 45% of thefts involved less than £100. The person most worried by becoming a victim of crime is usually female, middle-aged or elderly and quite well-off. In fact, the person most likely to be robbed is a young, working-class male.

## The public

Whatever the problems in deciding what the true picture is, crime is on the increase and people are more worried about it than they were years ago. Some people do not go out alone at night. Many more houses and cars are fitted with alarms. Popular 'Neighbourhood Watch' schemes have been encouraged by the police (Source 1).

## The police

With rising crime and fewer cases being solved, the police are under pressure. At the same time, they have less public support than they had in the early 20th century.

Middle-class property owners want less crime and blame the police for not catching burglars. At the same time, they may be resentful at being caught speeding or parking in the wrong place. Heavy-handed attempts to 'stop and search' youngsters may involve middle-class youngsters too. Their parents are likely to make more of a fuss about this than some working-class parents.

The black community, harassed by racist attacks, feels that the police have not taken them seriously. Racist attitudes were certainly to be found among the police, as a Police Research Institute survey of 1984 showed. However, the police have made concerted efforts to deal with racism and there is no general evidence that they respond to complaints from black citizens less readily than from white.

## Politics

Crime is now a major concern of many people and politicians have stepped into the discussion with vote-catching remedies. Labour leader Tony Blair's 1995 slogan 'Tough on crime, tough on the causes of crime' gained popular support.

The trouble is that, in politics, a slogan or a speech can be more important than following a policy through over several years to see if it brings results. This is particularly true of prison policy (see opposite page).

**SOURCE 1**

'Neighbourhood Watch' sign in a country village.

# PRISONS IN THE 20TH CENTURY

*KEY QUESTIONS*
◆ *Why has prison policy changed?*
◆ *What do we expect of our prisons?*

## Prison reform in the 20th century

As we saw on page 7 of this book, a prison sentence has several different purposes. It is designed to punish the criminal, deter others, satisfy the public and to change the inmate so that he or she does not commit any more crimes. It is hard to do all of these things at the same time, in the same place, and priority is usually given to one or the other aim. Prison policy in Britain has swung backwards and forwards between priorities.

After the Prisons Act of 1865, Prison Commissioner Edmund du Cane ran prisons on 'hard labour, hard fare and hard board' (see page 73). By the end of the century public opinion was turning against this approach. It was called 'a massive machine for the promotion of misery.' The famous writer, Oscar Wilde, served two years in prison (Source 1), and wrote in 'The Ballad of Reading Gaol':

> 'Something was dead in each of us,
> And what was dead was hope.'

Winston Churchill declared that: 'an important measure of a civilised country is how it treats its prisoners.'

### SOURCE 1

Prison life, with its endless restrictions makes one rebellious. The most terrible thing about it is not that it breaks one's heart, but that it turns one's heart to stone. It is only with a front of brass and a lip of scorn that one can get through the day.

*The famous playwright and poet, Oscar Wilde, served two years in Reading Gaol for homosexuality (1895–97). He wrote about his experiences.*

### SOURCE 2

Prison discipline should be designed to awaken prisoners' moral instincts, to train them in orderly and industrious habits, and, wherever possible, to turn them out of prison better men and women, physically and morally, than when they went in.

*From the Gladstone Report, 1895.*

The Gladstone Report, 1895, shows a swing towards reform (Source 2) and led to the 1898 Prisons Act. Du Cane retired and was replaced by two great reformers: Ruggles-Brise (1895–1921) then Sir Alexander Paterson (Source 3). Under these two men British prisons changed.

Shaven heads and the broad arrow uniform ended in 1921; prisoners were allowed to talk to each other at certain times ('association') from 1923. The first 'open prison' was set up at Wakefield in 1936. At an open prison, rules are more relaxed, prisoners work during the day, sometimes outside the prison. It is a preparation for life outside prison and is suitable for prisoners who are trying to 'go straight' and for prisoners near the end of their sentences.

The 1948 Criminal Justice Act abolished flogging and recommended more time on work training, learning a skill so that a prisoner could get a job on release and was not driven back to crime. There was also more psychiatric advice, better food, TV, and more prison visitors to befriend prisoners and keep them in touch with outside life. At this point those running British prisons really felt they were able to deal with all the different kinds of people who end up in prison, in a humane way, with a chance of reforming many of them.

## Avoiding prison

At the same time efforts were made to keep people out of prison: the **Probation Service** began in 1907. A convicted offender is attached to a probation officer who works with him or her to get their life in order and avoid crime.

In 1914 offenders were given time to pay their fine, instead of being sent to prison because they could not pay on the spot. The number of people in British prisons actually fell from 18,000 in 1900 to 11,000 in 1928.

In 1967 suspended sentences were introduced: the offender could avoid a prison sentence if he or she stayed out of trouble. In 1972 Community Service Orders were introduced; instead of being sent to prison, an offender had to do 40 to 120 hours unpaid work helping in the community, under the supervision of a probation officer. In 1982 Day Centres were set up. Offenders have to attend so many hours a week.

## The prison crisis

Since the 1950s prisons have found it increasingly hard to keep up the reforming approach which started with the Gladstone Report. At times there have been serious crises. There are several reasons for this:

**(a) Over-crowding.** The increase in crime, see page 89, has meant more people being sent to prison. The prison population has risen from 20,000 in 1950 to nearly 60,000 by 1997. British prisons only have room for 40,000. This means prisoners having to share cells, more squalid conditions, less time in the workshops, less attention to each prisoner, more time simply locked up. More new prisons are being built, but not fast enough for the rise in numbers.

**(b) Longer sentences.** In spite of recommendations to reduce the prison population, some politicians and judges have responded to the increase in crime by calling for, and giving, longer sentences. Ten years used to be a rare sentence; now 10, 15 or even 20 years are given for armed robbery or arson.

**(c) New types of prisoners.**
● **'Lifers'.** Among those who have long sentences are those sentenced to life imprisonment for murder following the abolition of the death penalty in 1965. There are now over 2,000 of these; they will normally serve at least ten years but for some life means life: they will never come out.

### SOURCE 3

You cannot train men for freedom in conditions of captivity.

*Prison Commissioner Sir Alexander Paterson, 1921.*

### SOURCE 4

Prisoners in Pentonville Prison in 1983 watching television during their 2 hours a week of being able to mix with other prisoners.

● **Terrorists.** Terrorist prisoners are given very long sentences: 35 years in some cases. This means they will be in prison longer than most lifers.

● **Sex offenders.** The numbers of sex offenders in prison has increased much faster than the number of other offenders. Other prisoners are extremely hostile to them and call them 'beasts'. They have to be locked up or kept separate from other prisoners for their own safety.

● **Escapes.** There have been a few sensational escapes from prison: George Blake, serving 42 years for spying, escaped from Wormwood Scrubs in 1966; two of the Great Train Robbers escaped; some IRA terrorists have escaped from high security prisons. These led to criticism that prisons were not even doing their main task: keeping people locked up. The Mountbatten Report on escapes grouped prisoners into four types, according to their likelihood of escaping. Category 'A' prisoners were to be kept in new Special Units in prisons, which cost £20,000 each to build.

All these factors have made prisons much harder to manage. Prisoners' resentment, which Oscar Wilde felt (Source 1), has turned to violence in a number of prison riots: in 41 prisons in 1971, in 1976 at Hull, in 1979 at Wormwood Scrubs for example. Most spectacular was in 1990 at Strangeways (Manchester), one of the biggest prisons in Europe, where rioting prisoners caused £60 million worth of damage (Source 6). Following the riot, the Woolf Report summed up the need for balance between the priorities (Source 7). However, with all the pressures on them it is hard for the prison service to find this balance.

## SOURCE 5

Inmates working on the prison farm at an open prison.

## SOURCE 6

Prisoners on the roof of Strangeways Prison, Manchester, April 1990.

## SOURCE 7

The prison service must set security, control and justice at the right level and it must provide the right balance between them. Security means the need to prevent prisoners escaping. Control means the duty to prevent prisoners causing a disturbance. Justice means the need to treat prisoners with humanity and fairness. The April riots occurred because these three elements were out of balance. These factors are dependent on each other. If there is an absence of justice, prisoners will be aggrieved. Control and security will be threatened.

*From the Woolf Report, 1990, written after riots at six prisons in April of that year, including a 25-day occupation of Strangeways Gaol, Manchester.*

## Prison policy in the 1990s

Since 1991, politicians have reacted to public worries over the level of crime by calling for more prison sentences and longer sentences. There was also a feeling that prisons were too 'soft'. The views of earlier prison commissioners like Paterson (Source 3), who also said that 'prison was the punishment, not a place of punishment' were overturned. The Conservative Home Secretary, Michael Howard, insisted that priority should be put on punishment, not reform. Less time and money was available for education, prison visitors, and talking to prisoners.

Private prisons, abolished in 1823, see page 71, were re-introduced. This is partly because the government wanted to break the power of the Prison Officers' union and partly because they wanted to set up prisons outside the control of Home Office civil servants, who, they felt, were too influenced by reformist ideas.

❖ *Look back over the story of prisons in Britain as told in this book (pages 70–75). Why does the pendulum keep swinging between reform and punishment?*
❖ *Are these changes good for prisons?*
❖ *Do you think tough prisons act as a deterrent to stop crime?*
❖ *Where would you put the priority: reform or punishment?*

# PROTEST: THE SUFFRAGETTES

## KEY QUESTIONS
◆ *Why did the suffragettes break the law?*
◆ *Did these tactics win the vote for women?*

Before the suffragettes, protest groups had usually tried to avoid breaking the law (like the 'moral' Chartists, page 82), or at least avoid getting caught (like the Luddites, page 80). The suffragettes decided that the best way of getting their message across was by deliberately breaking the law and being arrested. Since then, other groups, notably anti-nuclear campaigners and animal rights groups, have used the same tactics.

Women had not been treated equally with men for centuries, in the law (as we have seen repeatedly in this book), and in many other ways. By the late 19th century they had made some gains: the Married Women's Property Acts of 1870 and 1882 allowed them to keep their own incomes and property when they married; they could go to university, train and practise as a doctor, stand and vote in local elections. But the big prize of the vote (suffrage) for Parliament was still denied. Votes for women had been debated in Parliament every year since 1867, but each time the all-male House of Commons rejected it. For many women it was the key issue: if women could vote, they could pass laws to deal with all kinds of other issues concerning women's rights.

In 1897 all the local women's suffrage groups ('Suffragists') were combined in the National Union of Women's Suffrage Societies. The NUWSS had 500 branches and their tactics were peaceful: petitions, meetings, leaflets (see Source 1).

### SOURCE 1

A propaganda postcard calling for Votes for Women.

### SOURCE 2

For simply disturbing the meeting, I should not be imprisoned. I must use some certain means of getting arrested: I must 'insult' the police. Even with my arms helpless, I could commit what was technically an assault and so I found myself arrested and charged with 'spitting at a policeman'.

The next morning we found that the long, long newspaper silence about women's suffrage was broken.

*Christabel Pankhurst describes her first arrest in 1905.*

### SOURCE 3

Bad laws made without due authority ought not to be obeyed, but ought to be resisted by every honest man and woman. It is such laws that militant suffragettes have broken.

*Christabel Pankhurst, in court, explains her attitude to the law.*

### SOURCE 5

When the suffragettes began their campaign they were mistaken for featherheads, flibbertigibbets. Now that they have proved that they are in dead earnest, they have frightened the government, they have broken through the law, they have made 'Votes for women' practical politics.

*Daily Mirror, 1906.*

### SOURCE 4

## The suffragettes

The suffragists seemed to be getting nowhere. Some politicians were in favour of votes for women, but not a majority in any party. In 1903 Mrs Emmeline Pankhurst and her two daughters, Christabel and Sylvia, founded the Women's Social and Political Union (WSPU) in Manchester. They became known as 'suffragettes'. They decided to force the topic of votes for women into every newspaper so it could not be ignored. They started by going to political meetings and shouting out; they were banned. In 1905 Christabel therefore set out to get herself arrested (Source 2). Her trial gave her a chance to speak her views (Source 3).

The suffragettes moved to London in 1906 and stepped up their law-breaking by smashing windows, slashing paintings, chaining themselves to the railings in Downing Street and setting light to letter-boxes. When they were arrested they demanded to be treated as political prisoners. When this was refused they went on hunger strike and were forcibly fed, which was very painful.

Suffragettes were not always law-breakers. While Parliament was discussing votes for women they called off their violence and held legal demonstrations (Source 4). When they failed again to win the vote the suffragettes returned to violence. In 1913 a suffragette, Emily Wilding Davison, was killed while trying to stop the King's horse at the Derby. You can read in Source 6 that, in one newspaper at least, the suffragettes' tactics were not gaining support.

By 1914, when the First World War broke out, women had not won the vote. The suffragettes called off their campaign and supported the war effort. So did millions of women workers, in factories, in transport, in farming and as nurses (Source 7). Many showed that they could do jobs closed to women in peacetime.

In 1918 the vote was given to all men over 21 and some women over 30; in 1928 women gained the right to vote on the same basis as men.

### SOURCE 6

A deed of this kind, we need hardly say, is not likely to increase the popularity of any cause with the public. Reckless madness is not regarded as a qualification for the vote. There can be no doubt that yesterday's exhibition will do more harm than good to the cause of women's suffrage.

*From* The Times *newspaper, after the death of Emily Wilding Davison in 1913.*

### SOURCE 7

| JOB | 1914 | 1918 |
| --- | --- | --- |
| Munitions | 212,000 | 947,000 |
| Transport | 18,200 | 117,200 |
| Business | 505,200 | 934,500 |
| Farming | 190,000 | 228,000 |
| Industry | 2,178,600 | 2,970,600 |
| Domestic service | 1,658,000 | 1,250,000 |
| Nursing | 542,000 | 652,000 |

*Some women workers, 1914 and 1918.*

### SOURCE 8
A suffragette procession.

1. *Read Source 1. What arguments does it make in favour of votes for women?*
2. *Read Source 3. What is Christabel's attitude to the law?*
3. *Read Sources 2 and 3. How far does Source 3 explain the events described in Source 2?*
4. *Look at Sources 1, 2, 3 and 4. What do they tell you about how the suffragettes tried to win the vote for women?*
5. *Read Sources 5 and 6. Why do you think they reach different conclusions about the suffragettes?*
6. *Study Source 7. What do these figures tell us about women's work during the First World War?*
7. *'The suffragettes won the vote for women.' Use these sources and your own knowledge to explain how accurate you think this statement is.*

# PROTEST: THE GENERAL STRIKE, 1926

The London Dock Strike of 1889 (see page 85), started a huge increase in trade union membership among the mass of unskilled workers. By 1892 1.5 million people were members of a trade union; by 1910 there were 2.6 million and by 1914, 4.1 million. During the First World War employers co-operated with unions to keep up production. In 1919 there were 7.9 million trade unionists, including many more women than before.

Most of these people, and their leaders, saw unions as the best way of gaining a higher standard of living. They would go on strike if necessary, and there were some bitter strikes in 1911, 1912 and 1913, but they never intended to break the law. A few, however, called 'syndicalists', wanted to go further. They wanted to set up large unions, which would all go on strike together – a General Strike – bringing the whole country to a standstill. The government would become powerless to act and the workers could then take over.

## The General Strike: Long-term causes

After the First World War British industry was hard-hit by competition from other countries. Many workers faced wage cuts and longer hours. This was especially felt in the coal-mining industry where relations between mine-owners and miners were already bad.

**SOURCE 2**

A general strike is not an industrial dispute. It is a revolutionary movement, intended to inflict suffering upon the great mass of innocent persons.

*From the* Daily Mail *editorial which the printers refused to handle, 2 May 1926.*

**SOURCE 3**

The laws of England are the people's birthright. Those laws are in your keeping. You have made Parliament their guardian. The General Strike is a challenge to Parliament, and is the road to ruin.

*From a radio broadcast by Stanley Baldwin, 6 May 1926.*

**SOURCE 4**

The TUC does not challenge the constitution. Its sole aim is to secure for the miners a decent standard of life. There is no constitutional crisis.

*From a statement put out on the radio by the TUC on 7 May 1926.*

**SOURCE 1**
London bus during the General Strike.

The export price of coal fell from £4 a tonne in 1920 to £1.75 in 1921. To meet this fall in income the mine-owners forced the miners to accept a cut in pay and longer hours.

## Short-term causes

In 1925 the price of coal fell below £1 a tonne. Again the owners called for wage-cuts and longer hours. This time other unions supported the miners. The Prime Minister, Stanley Baldwin, gave a nine-month subsidy to keep up the miners' wages. Meanwhile he prepared for a general strike by setting up the OMS (Organisation for the Maintenance of Supplies). The TUC (Trade Union Congress) feared wage cuts throughout industry and prepared to support the miners. The subsidy ran out in May 1926. Discussions were held between the government and the TUC, but when some printers, without TUC backing, refused to print an anti-strike editorial (Source 2), Baldwin called them off.

## The Strike

The General Strike began on 4 May 1926. Four million trade unionists – miners, railwaymen, transport workers, builders, chemical workers, printers, engineers, gas workers and shipbuilders – came out on strike. The TUC did not ask public health, food or medical workers to strike.

Both sides now engaged in a propaganda battle (see Sources 1 to 7). The government tried to persuade the British people that the General Strike was not just a strike, but an attack on the laws and the constitution. The TUC tried to persuade them that it was not.

After only nine days, with the strike still solid and beginning to have real impact, the TUC called it off. The miners fought on alone, until they were driven back to work in 1927 by hunger. Trade union membership fell back below 4 million by 1930. There has never been a general strike in Britain since.

### SOURCE 5

A food convoy leaving London docks on 9 May 1926, with a military escort.

### SOURCE 6

Raising the siege at the docks. 20 armoured cars and 100 motor lorries. A long line of motor lorries swinging into Hyde Park during the weekend bore witness to the fact that the strikers had suffered an early defeat in their attempt to starve London.

*A description of the incident shown in Source 5.*

### SOURCE 7

I learnt from one of the dockers' pickets that about 150 tonnes of meat had been taken from one of the ships and was now being moved by this unnecessary display of force. The men, whose normal work is to handle thousands of tons of such cargo each day, lined the streets with arms folded, smiling and chatting, some waving a greeting to the soldiers.

*The TUC newspaper* British Worker *describes the incident shown in Source 5.*

1. *Look at Source 1.*
   *(i) What three unusual things can you see in this picture?*
   *(ii) Use your own knowledge to explain the reasons for each of them.*
2. *Read Source 2. Why did the printers refuse to print this article?*
3. *Read Source 3. In what ways does Source 3 agree with Source 2 about the strike?*
4. *Read Source 4. In what ways does Source 4 disagree with Sources 2 and 3 about the strike?*
5. *Look at Source 5 and read Source 6. Was the writer of Source 6 a supporter of the strikers? Use your knowledge of the General Strike to explain your answer.*
6. *Read Source 7. In what ways does this Source give a different view of the events shown in Source 5 from Source 6?*
7. *Which of Sources 5, 6 or 7 is the most useful for finding out about the General Strike? Explain your answer.*
8. *After reading all about the General Strike in the Sources and text, do you think it was a 'challenge to the laws'? Use these Sources and your own knowledge to explain your answer.*

# PROTEST: CONSCIENTIOUS OBJECTORS

*KEY QUESTION*
◆ *Should people who object to a law be made to obey it?*

The state makes the laws. A citizen has to obey the laws. But what if a citizen thinks the law is wrong?

**The State says:** we have passed this law for the good of the people as a whole; you must obey it.

**The citizen says:** my conscience tells me this law is wrong, but I will obey it because I belong to this society and so must accept its rules.

But suppose we push this situation to extremes? What if the state asks you to kill another human being? For some people, the state has gone too far: their consciences object to their doing it. They are conscientious objectors.

In previous wars the problem did not arise: armies were made up of volunteers. In this century, in both world wars, the British government introduced conscription. In other words, everyone in certain groups would be called up to fight. Let us look at how Conscientious Objectors (COs) were treated in each war.

## The First World War

The long-drawn out struggle of the First World War demanded more soldiers than Britain had ever mobilised before. Huge efforts were made to persuade men to volunteer and the country was in a frenzy of patriotism. However, by 1916 still more men were needed and conscription was introduced by law in January: every unmarried man between 18 and 41 was called up. In April this was extended to married men.

Quaker MPs had put a clause into the law that allowed people who objected to military service on grounds of conscience to be let off. There were two types of COs: religious pacifists, who took literally the Biblical commandment 'Thou shalt not kill', and Socialists, whose objection to the war is given in Source 1. In fact, some people belonged to both groups.

They had to appear before a tribunal to state their case. Public opinion was hostile to COs and this was reflected in the tribunals. They sometimes included retired soldiers and were often unsympathetic both to socialism and pacifism (Source 2). Of 14,000 COs who went before tribunals only 400 were given absolute exemption from the war. Another 6,000 were sent to do 'work of national importance', such as farming, mining, or hospital work, 5,000 were given non-fighting duties in the army and 2,600 had their case completely rejected.

Of the 13,600, over 6,000 refused to accept the tribunal's decision. They argued that even 'work of national importance' or non-fighting duties would still be helping the war effort. Many were put in prison, often in solitary confinement (Source 3). Many were treated as if they had been called up into the army. COs refused to wear uniform, obey any orders, etc. As soldiers disobeying orders, they were subject to harsh punishments: for example, John Brightmore was made to stand in a waterlogged hole, 10 feet deep, for several days. Some were sent to France, nearer to the fighting. Punishments were more severe in this situation, including the firing squad (Source 4).

Only 351 COs gave in under this pressure and the army soon realised they were wasting their time. The COs were then handed over to the civilian authorities and given long prison sentences with hard labour (Source 5). By the end of the war 73 COs had died as a result of their treatment and 31 had been driven insane. Those who survived lost the right to vote for five years.

### SOURCE 1

*As war breaks out in August 1914, the Independent Labour Party explains why socialists would not fight:*

Out of the darkness we hail our working-class comrades of every land. Across the roar of guns we send sympathy and greetings to the German Socialists. They are no enemies of ours, but faithful friends.

### SOURCE 2

(a) Chairman of the Wirral Tribunal: 'I wish the government had not put in this clause about conscientious objectors. I don't agree with it myself.'

(b) A Councillor at Shaw, Manchester: 'I think you are exploiting God to save your own skin. A man who would not help to defend his country and womankind is a coward and a cad. You are nothing but a shivering mass of unwholesome fat.'

*The tribunals in action, 1916.*

Conscientious objectors at Dyce Quarry Home Office Work Centre, Aberdeenshire.

## SOURCE 3

'That strength enables me to firmer stand

Than ever in the cause of truth; for laws

Of right, 'gainst those of might; at His command

I turn again unwounded to the strife

Against war, for love – Nay more,'gainst death, for life.'

*An extract from a poem written by a religious conscientious objector, Harry Stanton, in Harwich Prison, in 1916, in which he calls on God to give him strength to keep going.*

## SOURCE 4

The soldiers began to form themselves into a kind of huge square until several thousand were present. There was a hush and the Adjutant read out the sentence: 'Private Marten, tried by Field Court Martial for disobedience. Sentenced to death by being shot. [Here a pause] Confirmed by General Sir Douglas Haig. [A longer pause] And commuted to ten years' penal servitude.

*Howard Marten, taken from Harwich Prison to France, hears his own death sentence read out to him.*

## The Second World War

The enormous slaughter of soldiers in the First World War led to an increase in the number of pacifists between the wars. The treatment COs had received, and their steadfastness in enduring it, also gained respect for Conscientious Objection. When conscription was introduced in 1939, COs were treated very differently. 59,162 people, this time including women, registered as COs. Tribunals were not allowed to include ex-soldiers and had to be more representative of all social classes. They were more understanding and acted much more carefully. COs might have been sacked, criticised in the newspapers, cursed by neighbours, but none suffered in the way they had in the First War.

❖ *Should there be a right of conscientious objection?*
❖ *Could this right go beyond refusing to fight? For example, some COs now object to paying taxes for the government to spend on nuclear weapons.*
❖ *Is there a 'higher law', a principle which is more important than the laws of the land? Can you give an example?*

# THE ROLE OF AN INDIVIDUAL: ELIZABETH FRY

*KEY QUESTION*
◆ *How did Elizabeth Fry change prisons?*

## Women's prisons in 1800

Early 19th century prisons were dreadful places (see page 69), but women's prisons were possibly worse than men's. The buildings were just as unsuitable, unhygienic and unhealthy. They had the same chaotic mixing of inmates, with those simply awaiting trial mingling with hardened criminals. Women prisoners were just as dependent on the gaoler for everything. Women's prisons usually had male gaolers, who often exploited the women.

But women convicts were the outcasts of society. The ideal woman of the time was an angel, a home-builder, wife and mother, gentle and virtuous. Women in prison had obviously broken this code. Few people pitied them. However, there was no shortage of women prisoners. In general, far fewer women than men committed crimes, but for some offences, like drunkenness, numbers of women and men were equal, and they were not far behind in murder. Four times more women were in prison, in proportion to the population, than today.

**SOURCE 1**

Elizabeth Fry in 19th-century Quaker dress.

## Elizabeth Fry (1780–1845)

Elizabeth Fry was the daughter of well-off Quakers in Norwich and married into a Quaker banking family. Her parents were not strict, and as a girl she wore the fashionable dresses of any girl from a rich family. But at about 18 she began to take her religion more seriously. One sign of this was her adoption of the simple Quaker dress and bonnet (Source 1).

Quakers have no paid ministers or clergy; anyone, man or woman, can speak at a Meeting for Worship, so Quaker women were more liberated than most at that time. Quakers also believe that there is something of God in everyone, and that has drawn many into working with prisoners. This wish to do something practical with her powerful religious beliefs led Elizabeth to visit the women's section of Newgate Prison just before Christmas 1813.

She was amazed at what she saw. A riotous, rowdy, screaming mass of 300 women were crammed into three rooms. Some were ill, but could not afford treatment; some were freezing cold but could not afford to pay for bedding; some were fighting; there were many children among them. She never forgot the sight of two women tearing the clothes off a dead baby to wrap around a live child. She returned the next day, with baby clothes and clean straw bedding. After these had been handed out she began to pray and many women around her joined in.

It was not until 1816 that she was able to return to Newgate. The chaplain and the gaoler both warned against going in. This time she simply appealed to the women to do something for their children. Her lack of fear and her directness made a huge impression and they started a school for the prison children.

Elizabeth Fry formed a group of mainly Quaker women to visit the prison daily and make changes to the way it was run. A matron was appointed to run the women's section, the women were supplied with materials to work at sewing or knitting to be sold and Bible readings were held.

She was asked to give evidence to a Parliamentary Committee in 1818, chaired by her brother-in-law. It reported that her efforts had made the women's section of Newgate an orderly, sober place, 'like a factory or a family'.

**SOURCE 4**

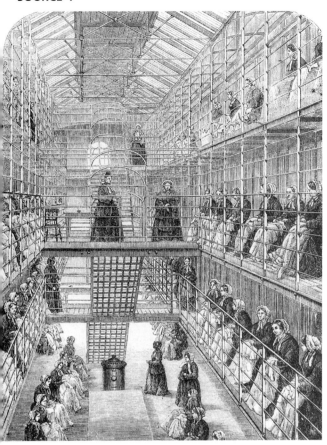

A women's prison in about 1870.

## Elizabeth Fry's influence in her own lifetime

Her fearlessness in working with women prisoners, her religious motives and her success made her famous. Her book, *Observations On Visiting, Superintendance And Government Of Female Prisons*, was published in 1827. She was always being asked to address meetings and was summoned to meet Queen Victoria in 1840.

Peel's Gaols Act of 1823 took up many of her ideas: gaolers had to be paid, prisoners were to be separated into categories and women had to have female gaolers and warders. However, Elizabeth was disappointed at how weak the Act was, with no effort at forcing all prisons to try to reform their inmates. Her own reforms cost money and she knew many prisons would not take them up unless they had to.

Her ideas struck a chord abroad, where women from Paris to St Petersburg formed prison visiting committees. Later in life she travelled widely in Europe. Everywhere, especially in France and Ireland, she was welcomed and listened to with respect.

## Opposition in England

In England, however, the tide was turning against her. The latest trend was towards punishment through strict isolation or hard labour (see page 73). Edwin Chadwick sneered at her and John Howard, although he had no evidence for the claim he makes in Source 2. The work Elizabeth gave her women was intended to give them a sense of dignity and perhaps an honest skill, not to break their spirits (Source 3). She spoke out against the cruelty of the Separate System.

**SOURCE 2**

Because of the Howards and Frys, the prisons had been so reformed by narrow sentiment and blind zeal as actually to attract vagrants and others who preferred their comfort to labour.

*Edwin Chadwick comments on John Howard and Elizabeth Fry.*

**SOURCE 3**

*Elizabeth Fry was said to be:*

Committed to reforming the prisoners by work, rather than punishing them by labour.

She was also in trouble in 1828, when her husband's bank went broke. She was accused of hypocrisy, of neglecting her family (she had 11 children), and of spending her husband's money on charity work in order to become famous. Some people were glad to see a woman reformer in an uncomfortable situation.

## Her long-term influence

When she died in 1845 prison regimes in England were not what she wanted them to be. Times had moved on, and the casual days when an upper-class lady could wander into a gaol and begin to meddle in how it was run were over. However, three ideas still present in British prisons owe their origins to Elizabeth Fry:

● Separate women's prisons, with a female staff.

● Volunteer prison visitors.

● A belief that prison is a place from which human beings can emerge better people than when they went in.

❖ Read again the sections in Chapter 5 about crime and prison reform. How would you explain:
  (i) Why Elizabeth Fry was a 19th-century heroine?
  (ii) Why her ideas were not actually taken up in full?

❖ Prisons are run by the state; it is hard for an individual to affect them. How much does 19th-century prison reform owe to Elizabeth Fry, and how much to other factors?

# ADULTS AND CHILDREN: YOUNG OFFENDERS

## KEY QUESTION

◆ *Should children who break the law be treated differently from adults?*

Children have always committed crimes. In the villages in which most people lived in the past, no doubt the farmer whose apples had been stolen by children dealt with them personally. Perhaps the farmer would go and complain to the delinquent children's parents. Perhaps the village constable gave them a severe telling off or clip on the ear. Only the most difficult and persistent child criminal got to court. When they did, they were punished as if they were adults. Children were put in prison, transported, even hanged. In 1880 there were 6,500 children under 16 in adult prisons, of whom 900 were under 12.

## The start of separate treatment for children

Children in cities may always have been different (for example, see Source 1, page 52). Certainly Dickens shocked Victorian Britain with his description of the Artful Dodger, and Fagin's trained gang of pickpockets (Source 1). *Oliver Twist* was fiction, but it was successful in getting people thinking about child crime and how to deal with it. There was a growing understanding that children were not just miniature adults, but developing human beings who were influenced by their environment. 19th-century reformers like Mary Carpenter asked some important questions:

● How and when does a child know what is right and wrong?

● What should be done about the fact that criminal and deprived backgrounds produced more child criminals?

● Children were likely to become criminals by sending them to an adult prison. What alternatives should there be?

## SOURCE 1

What was Oliver's horror and alarm as he stood a few paces off . . . to see the Dodger plunge his hand into the gentleman's pocket, and draw from thence a handkerchief; to see him hand the same to Charley Bates; and finally to behold them both running away around the corner at full speed!

*From Charles Dickens'* Oliver Twist, *1837. The innocent orphan, Oliver Twist, sees the boy pickpockets of Fagin's gang, Charley Bates and the 'Artful Dodger', at work for the first time.*

In 1854 Reformatory Schools were set up. Someone under 16 would do two weeks in a prison (perhaps as a shock?), then go to one of these schools for at least two years. They were very tough (Source 2), but the clear intention was to separate a child from his or her bad home environment.

## SOURCE 2

*The Reverend Sydney Turner was in charge of Redhill Reformatory in the late 19th century and believed in severely punishing boys by locking them up alone:*

. . . for a few days in unheated cells on a bread and water diet and by whipping them with as much solemnity and form as possible.

In 1902 an experimental school to try to reform repeating offenders aged 15–21 was started at Borstal, in Kent. It was run like a public school, with lots of sport and residential houses. The idea was to take the young offender away from bad influences at home and give him or her clear guidance and a new chance. Youngsters and staff did not wear uniform and the length of their sentence depended on how the youngster was getting on, reviewed every month. The plan for more such schools, called Borstals, was extended in 1908 and for a time they were very successful.

In 1932 Reformatory Schools were replaced by Approved Schools for offenders under 15. A total of 86 boys' schools and 35 girls' schools were set up.

The **1908 Children's Act** was an important move in the separate treatment of children. It stopped children under 14 being sent to prison and created special Juvenile Courts, distinct from the regular magistrates' courts.

## SOURCE 3

The importance of the impact on offenders of the first few days of a detention centre sentence has been confirmed . . . so the initial two-week programme will be particularly brisk. Greater emphasis will be placed on parades and inspections. High standards of cleanliness, tidiness, discipline and personal effort will be required.

*Leon Brittan, Home Secretary in 1985, describes how he wanted Detention Centres to be run.*

SOURCE 4
A new inmate arrives at a Youth Custody Centre.

After 1908 a child under seven was held not to be responsible for his or her actions: the 'age of criminal responsibility'. This was raised to eight in 1933 and to 10 in 1963.

## Today

Juvenile Courts still exist. While trying to keep the court small and informal, there are always representatives of the offender's school and home, so that the JPs have a full picture of the child they are judging.

They have a large number of options before them, ranging from quite harsh punishments to careful efforts to get the child to stay out of trouble.

**(i) Care.** They can bind the parents over to control the child, or take the child away from the parental home into care, or have the child supervised by a probation officer.

**(ii) Non-custodial sentences** (i.e. not locking the child up). Putting the child in care; fining the parents, perhaps with the fine being paid to the victim; probation; Attendance Centre (see below); Community Service Order (see below).

**(iii) Custodial sentences.** Detention Centre (see below) or Youth Custody (see below).

**Attendance Centre.** These were set up in 1948. 10–21 year-olds have to attend each Saturday for 2–3 hours, up to a total of 36 hours for 17–21 year-olds. Used for more serious offenders who have broken probation. The next step is a custodial sentence.

**Community Service Order.** From 1972, 16–18 year-olds can be made to do useful work in the community, up to a maximum of 120 hours. This has been very successful with some offenders and is cheap to run.

**Approved Schools and Borstals.** Research showed that 60% of those who left approved schools between 1963 and 1967 offended again. They were abolished in 1969. Of those who left Borstals in 1975, 85% re-offended. They were abolished in 1982 and Juvenile Courts could sentence young offenders to Detention Centre or Youth Custody instead.

**Detention Centre.** These were set up in 1948 and the aim was to give young offenders aged 14–21 a 'short, sharp shock'. They were sentenced to 3 to 16 weeks, with lots of drill and military-style discipline. Various Home Secretaries have said they will tighten up the rules (see Source 3). This policy is appealing to some voters, but it seems not to work with offenders: 75% of those who left in 1975 offended again.

**Youth Custody.** Rather longer sentences, of 4 to 12 months, for boys aged 15–20 and girls aged 17–20. Many offenders have committed acts of violence, or are drug addicts, or are immature with no employable skills. It is a punishment, but offenders are also expected to learn self-discipline and self-control.

❖ *(i) How does a child learn the difference between right and wrong?*
*(ii) At what age does a child know that stealing is a crime?*

❖ *'Young offenders get off lightly.'*
*(i) Which of the sentencing options described above would you regard as 'light'?*
*(ii) Do you agree with the statement above?*

❖ *'The short, sharp shock does more for the popularity of politicians than for the offender.' Explain why you agree or disagree with this statement.*

❖ *Why do most of the attempts to punish, deter or reform young offenders seem to have failed?*

# IDEAS ABOUT WHAT IS A CRIME: THE TOLPUDDLE MARTYRS

## KEY QUESTION

◆ *Why did trade unions need changes in the law in order to get started?*

The law has always found it difficult to deal with trade unions. In law, each employee makes an individual contract with the employer, as equals. In fact, of course, they are far from equal. The employer can increase hours, reduce wages, operate unsafe conditions and the employee can either put up with it or quit. To leave, in times of high unemployment, could mean to starve. The worker will simply be replaced by someone who will put up with these conditions.

The only way an employee can increase his or her bargaining power is to act together with other workers. Together they can make their employer listen to them because they cannot all be sacked at once. This needs organisation, and that is what trade unions are for. It also means that, to be effective, the union must have the support of most of the workers. This is not easy to achieve. The impact on the rights of other workers, and the reasons for it, are described in Source 1.

During the early 19th century, when workers' need for protection was at its greatest, it was hard to get unions organised. The law was often used against them by government and employers.

## SOURCE 1

*In this extract, adapted from* North and South, *a novel published in 1854 by Mrs Gaskell, a worker describes the Union at his cotton factory to a woman questioner:*

Well, if a man doesn't belong to the Union, those that work the looms next to him have orders not to speak to him. He's out of bounds. He comes among us, he works among us, but he's not of us. In some places you can be fined for speaking to him. You try that, miss. Try living a year or two among people who look away if you look at them, and you'll know a bit about what the union is.

*[The woman complains that this is like a torture.]*
You can say what you like. Unions began in days of sore depression; it was a necessity. It's a necessity now. It's to withstand injustice, past, present or to come. Our only chance is binding men together in one common interest; and if some are cowards and some are fools, they must come along and join the great march, whose only strength is numbers.

## The Tolpuddle Martyrs

In 1833, in Dorset, farmworkers' wages were cut from 9/- (45p) to 7/- (35p) a week. When there was a proposal to cut wages further, to 6/- (30p), six of them met together in the village of Tolpuddle.

What could they do? There had been outbreaks of rural violence in 1830 – the Captain Swing Riots (see page 81) – which had been brutally suppressed. They agreed that it was impossible to live and feed their families on the reduced wages without turning to crime. They were responsible men: their leader, George Loveless, was a Methodist lay preacher. He knew that trade unions were legal so he formed the Friendly Society of Agricultural Labourers to press their case to the farmers in a united but peaceful way. They knew that the farmers, and their friends among the magistrates, would be hostile so they took a secret oath not to reveal who they were.

Trade unions were indeed legal at that time. Robert Owen had just set up the Grand National Consolidated Trade Union, with half a million members all over the country. But the government was determined to crush them. When local magistrates in Dorset wrote to the Home Secretary, Lord Melbourne, telling him about unions being set up there, they were encouraged to act ruthlessly. Melbourne suggested the law under which they could be prosecuted. George Loveless, his brother James and four other Tolpuddle labourers were put on trial in February 1834.

They were tried under a law of 1797, which made it illegal to take secret oaths. This had originally been passed to prevent mutinies in the navy during the Napoleonic Wars. In spite of George Loveless' spirited defence (Source 2), the judge was clearly determined to convict them and they were sentenced to seven years' transportation.

Many in the ruling classes applauded (Source 3). However, there were huge protests (Source 4). Within two years the Tolpuddle Martyrs had been pardoned.

## SOURCE 2

My Lord, if we have broken the law it was not done intentionally. We have injured no man's character, reputation, person or property. We were uniting together to preserve ourselves, our wives and our children from utter degradation and starvation.

*George Loveless to the judge at his trial.*

Mass meeting to protest at the transportation of the Tolpuddle Martyrs, 1834.

## SOURCE 3

The leaders of these unions are, for the most part, selfish, worthless and designing men. These men care not a straw for the working classes . . . such are the criminals whom it would be justice to attack, and a public benefit to punish.

*From* The Times, *April 1834.*

## The right to join a union

It was nearly 40 years before the legal position of trade unions was improved. In the case of Hornby *v.* Close, 1867, the Bradford Boilermakers' Union was not allowed to sue their treasurer who had stolen £24 from them because, in law, a trade union was not allowed to exist. Further, **picketing** (putting pressure on other workers not to go to work during a strike) was regarded as a crime by many magistrates.

Then came two important acts:

● 1872 Trade Union Act, made trade unions legal.

● 1875 Trade Union Act, legalised peaceful picketing.

This led to an increase in trade union membership: there were 4.1 million trade unionists by 1914 and by 1970 more than half of all working people were in a union.

In the 1970s and 1980s the law on trade unions was changed, and is still controversial. Each year there is a rally at Tolpuddle to commemorate the six men who suffered for the right of a worker to join a trade union. (See also page 84 for more on trade unions, page 102 on the General Strike.)

❖ *Trade unions have never lived easily inside the law because of a clash between the demands of the trade union and the rights of an individual. Explain how the rights of*
*(i) an individual worker and*
*(ii) the rights of an employer to run his or her business the way they want to, might clash with the way a trade union has to operate.*
❖ *Why are the Tolpuddle labourers called 'Martyrs'?*
❖ *'Trade unions: Vital protection for the worker or An infringement on individual liberty?'*
*What is your view on this controversy?*

# ECONOMIC AND SOCIAL PRESSURES: THE REBECCA RIOTS

## KEY QUESTION

◆ **What part did economic difficulties play in the Rebecca Riots?**

The Rebecca Riots took place in west Wales in the years 1839–1843. Large gangs of poor farmers attacked turnpike tollgates; their leaders dressed in women's clothing and took the name 'Rebecca'. Why did they attack tollgates? And why did they dress up?

Some people in desperate economic difficulties turn to crime. Others, as we have seen in this book, turn to organised protest (see especially Source 1 on page 77 for the link between hard times and protest). Unlike farmers in much of England, farmers in west Wales were poor (Source 1). Their income, from a small farm of about 50 acres (20 hectares), might be £180 in a good year. Their expenditure was:

| | |
|---|---|
| Rent | £60 |
| Tithes | £9 |
| Wages for 2 workers @ £25 a year each: | £50 |
| Rates | £2 |
| Tolls | £9 |
| Total | £130 |

The farmers were angry about several of these items:

● rents were very high because there were lots of people wanting to rent land. Most of the landowners were English.

● Tithes went to the Church of England, although most

## SOURCE 1

A poor Welsh farm in the 19th century.

farmers did not go to the Church but to the Methodist or Baptist chapels. Before 1839 tithes could be paid in farm produce, but now they had to be paid in cash.

● The rates included church rate (which they resented for the same reason), poor rate and road rate. They did not like the new Poor Law of 1834, which set up workhouses in the local town of Carmarthen, and the poor rate which went towards building them. They resented having to pay a road rate, for local roads, as well as tolls on the main roads.

● These tolls were the last straw. To improve the land on their hilly farms they spread lime on it. This had to be brought from south Wales. The main roads had been taken over by a turnpike trust, which raised money to improve them by building gates at regular intervals and charging a toll to go through them. Sometimes the gatekeepers would let the farmers off as they were local and regular users, but in 1839 a new man, an Englishman, took on the gates. He had paid a fixed sum to the turnpike trust and collected as much for himself as possible from the tolls. He also put up four new gates.

A cartoon from 1843 shows the range of grievances of the Rebecca rioters.

## SOURCE 2

## Why Rebecca?

One dark night in 1839 a group of farmers got together and destroyed one of the tollgates. It was re-built and destroyed again. The magistrates called in constables and even 25 soldiers. The farmers knew that the punishments, if they were caught, were serious. On the third raid the leader decided to disguise himself a bit and put on a dress belonging to a woman called Rebecca. That is one reason for the name; the other is a verse from the Bible: 'And they blessed Rebecca and said to her, be the mother of thousands of millions and let your children possess the gates of those which hate them.'

In the end the magistrates ordered the gate not to be re-built and the new ones to be taken down.

The harvests of 1839, 1840 and 1841 were bad. The farmers faced starvation. The 1842 harvest was better, but prices for their corn, barley and butter were low. By next spring the farmers were angry and desperate. By May 1843 20 tollgates had been destroyed. In each case the leader was dressed as 'Rebecca'. Most were in remote country areas but one was the Water Street Gate in Carmarthen (Source 3).

### SOURCE 3

May 27. About one o'clock this morning Rebecca and her sister Charlotte, together with about 300 of the children, paid a visit to Water Street Gate, and in about 20 minutes the two thick oak posts had been sawn off close to the ground, the gate smashed to pieces, the lamp post destroyed, the glass in the windows broken and the tiled roof stripped.

*Nearly 50 years later, Alcwyn Evans remembers the attack on the Water Street Gate in Carmarthen in 1843.*

## Social pressures

The cartoon (Source 2) shows that the attacks on tollgates were part of wider grievances. As the summer of 1843 went on 'Rebecca' turned on other targets: farmers who had more than one farm, men who had fathered babies but refused to marry the mother, wife-beaters and fathers who had deserted their families. For a while 'Rebecca' made the laws and represented community feelings. Some idea of this social pressure can be read in Source 4.

The magistrates were powerless. It was a remote area and they were mostly outsiders, usually English-speaking. In June they had to call in a regiment of cavalry from Cardiff. The meeting referred to in Source 4 led to an attack on the Carmarthen workhouse, but the soldiers drove them off. In

### SOURCE 4

*On 18 June 1843 this notice was posted, in Welsh, on the door of every chapel and church for miles around Carmarthen; the translation is:*

If you call yourself a man not a boy of 16 or a dodderer over 70, make sure you come to the 'Plough and Harrow' next Monday morning, to pay a little visit to the mayor in Carmarthen. If you are not there, you need show no surprise when your house burns down in the middle of the night.

Remember the warning of

'Becca.'

September, following a tip-off, the soldiers captured seven rioters, including their 'Rebecca', Jac Ty-Isha. In the same week a 75-year-old tollgate keeper was shot dead during a Rebecca attack. The jury dared not return a verdict of murder for fear of reprisals. Criminals began to use the 'Rebecca' disguise and it was clear that things were getting out of hand.

Over the summer several Welsh Chartists (see page 82) had addressed huge meetings in the area. The farmers were persuaded to put their grievances in a petition to the government, which set up an enquiry. It recommended that:

- the toll system should be reformed so that the farmers paid less;

- tithes should be reduced (although the chapel-going farmers still had to pay them until 1918);

- rents should be reduced;

- there should be more Welsh-speaking magistrates (although Welsh could not be used in law-courts for another hundred years).

Jac Ty-Isha was sentenced to 20 years' transportation to Australia.

❖ *(i) List the long-term economic difficulties of the small farmers in west Wales.*
*(ii) What other causes of hardship did they face which were not economic?*
*(iii) What economic difficulties triggered the outbreak of the Rebecca Riots in 1843?*
❖ *Write up your answer to the question 'What were the causes of the Rebecca riots?'*
*Here are your paragraph headings:*
*The long-term economic causes of the riots were ...*
*The non-economic causes were ...*
*The short-term economic causes were ...*
❖ *How were people put under pressure to join, or support, the Rebecca Riots?*

# PROPERTY LAWS: POACHING AND WRECKING

## KEY QUESTION
◆ *Should we feel sorry for poachers?*

Deer, hares, rabbits, pigeons, pheasants, partridges, ducks, swans, fish are all wild creatures. However, from way back in medieval times, the upper classes had regarded them as their property, to hunt as they wished. One of the crimes of Robin Hood (see page 28) was killing the king's deer, and laws against poaching date back to 1389. With the victory of the landowning classes over both the king and the lower classes in the 17th century, these property rights were forcefully protected.

The 1671 Game Act said that only those owning freehold land worth £100 a year, or holding a 99-year lease on land worth £150 a year, or the son and heir of such a property-owner, could hunt the creatures listed above. In other words, those creatures were the property of better-off landowners and to kill them was the crime of poaching. This applied even if they were on your own land. Other laws backed this up: you could be fined £5 for having a hunting dog, or a snare, and £30 for killing a deer. In 1723 the 'Black Act' made it a serious offence to poach with a blackened face. Poachers had up before the local JP stood little chance of getting off lightly: most JPs, clergy included, were keen hunters and jealously protected their sport. Only one witness was needed for a conviction, usually a gamekeeper, few cases went to trial by jury and some were settled by one JP on his own.

## SOURCE 1

Many people refused to treat the poacher as an ordinary criminal. The working class regarded certain kinds of poachers as popular heroes. They rescued them from the hands of keepers and police and intimidated those people who took them to court.

*A modern historian, D. Jones, describes poaching as a 'social crime'.*

## SOURCE 2

The general opinion is that game is not private property. They say that God has made the game of the land free, and left it free.

*A Berkshire JP, 1826.*

## SOURCE 3

A mantrap (illegal from the 1830s, but still used long afterwards).

Many historians regard poaching as a classic example of a 'social crime' (see Source 1 and page 55). That is, many people refused to accept the idea that wild creatures were the sole property of rich landowners. Some of these animals destroyed their crops too, yet they were not allowed to touch them. Many were good to eat, especially for hungry and poorly-paid farm labourers. In Cannock Chase, local people felt they had the right to take animals on what they regarded as common land. When the Earl of Uxbridge tried to set up rabbit-farming on the Chase as a commercial business in 1753 200 local people dug up the warrens with spades. It took two weeks. A local farmer roasted an ox and provided them with bread and cheese and they made every effort to act as if they were the forces of law acting against a law-breaker.

In the 19th century the situation worsened. Farm labourers were worse off. Some landowners turned their estates into game preserves. New methods of dealing with poachers were introduced, such as automatic spring guns and mantraps (Source 3). Poaching carried a maximum sentence of 14 years' transportation. Farm labourers begrudged the fact that pheasant chicks were fed on boiled eggs while their own children went hungry. In 1862 someone suspected of poaching could be stopped and searched, even in their own homes. The situation was slightly improved in 1883, when tenants were allowed to trap rabbits and hares on their own farms.

## A social crime?

Traditionally, therefore, most poachers have been seen as poor people, supplementing their diet with the odd poached animal. It was also seen as a harmless contest, using your knowledge and skill to outwit the gamekeepers. How accurate is this interpretation?

**a) Gentlemen poachers.** The legal records show that quite a few poachers were not poor farm labourers. In 1796 the Rev. Francis Barstow was fined £20 for shooting game without a licence. 15% of those involved in the Cannock Chase attacks on the Earl of Uxbridge's game were gentlemen. Clearly those prevented from hunting under the terms of the 1671 Game Act included quite well-off farmers who resented the rules as much as the poor.

**b) Poaching for sale.** Poaching was a well-organised business. Men like John Lightwood, who took 80 hares in the winter of 1764, and sold them at 3/-(15p) each (= £12, a year's wages), and Edward Tunbridge (Source 4) were not just feeding their families. In fact there was a strong demand for game, particularly

### SOURCE 4

He hath for more than twenty years continually abused me and others, and still does, in stealing my conies [rabbits], robbing my fishponds, and taking my partridges and pheasants. [As a result] my conies are stolen so that I cannot serve any in my house, my ponds which I stored for the provision of my house are robbed, most of my partridges and pheasants he hath not left any.

*Poaching in 16th-century Essex: in 1598 Francis Harvey JP complained about a persistent poacher, Edward Tunbridge.*

### SOURCE 5

We pray thee, O Lord, not that wrecks should happen, but that, if wrecks do happen Thou wilt guide them into the Scilly Isles, for the benefit of the poor inhabitants.

*The 'wreckers' prayer', from the Isles of Scilly.*

among the middle classes in towns, which local butchers tried to meet. An Act of 1707 made it illegal to trade in game but there was a flourishing black market. Many poachers made it their way of life and some poaching gangs were large and well-organised.

**c) Violence.** With large profits involved, violence between poachers and gamekeepers is more understandable. In 1844 30 gamekeepers were killed in Gloucestershire alone. This kind of civil war is not the traditional image of poaching.

## Wrecking

KEY QUESTION
◆ *Was wrecking a social crime?*

The law on shipwrecks was quite clear. It dated back to Henry II: the ship and its goods were the property of the shipowner and the merchant. If no one claimed them for a year and a day they belonged to the monarch.

Unfortunately, the people who lived on the coasts of Cornwall, the Scilly Isles, Wales and the Wirral had different views. They believed that one-third of all the goods and timber from a shipwreck belonged to them. In 1740, in the Wirral, local people took 3,000 barrels of brandy from the cargo of 9,000 barrels on a shipwreck, taking it home in saucepans, kettles and anything else they could find. The lives of the islanders on the almost treeless Scillies depended on what they called 'wreckwood' (Source 5). Ships which were only aground, and could have been floated off at the next high tide, were often quickly pillaged before it came. As British trade expanded in the 18th century more ships were wrecked. A new law was passed against wreckers in 1753, but it did little to change attitudes.

❖ *Describe the traditional view of the poacher, in three short sentences.*
❖ *How do the three points made here (a)–(c) affect that description?*
❖ *Write your own brief, accurate account of poaching in the 18th and 19th centuries.*
❖ *Do you think*
  *(i) poaching and*
  *(ii) wrecking were 'social crimes'?*

# GOVERNMENT ACTION: LAWS AGAINST DISCRIMINATION

*KEY QUESTION*
◆ *Can laws change attitudes?*

Government action has been the key factor affecting crime, punishment and protest. In this book, we have seen that:

● The first governments enforced the first codes of laws (see Chapter 1).

● Medieval monarchs tried to offer better justice than barons or manor courts (see Chapter 2, pages 20–21).

● Governments have decided what punishments there should be. See, for example, the 'Bloody Code' (Chapter 3, pages 50–51) and transportation (page 69).

● Governments have created some crimes, such as smuggling (see Chapter 3, pages 54–55).

● Many forms of protest have been directed against the government, such as the Pilgrimage of Grace and Kett's Rebellion (Chapter 3, pages 39–41), the Gunpowder Plot (Chapter 3, page 45), Peterloo and Chartism (Chapter 4, pages 78–79 and 82–83) and the Suffragettes (Chapter 5, pages 100–101).

● Governments have played an even bigger part in crime and punishment in recent centuries. See, for example, government take-over of prisons (Chapter 4, page 73), and the growth of the police force (page 120).

● Governments have met new situations by passing laws which create new crimes, such as motoring offences (Chapter 5, page 90).

Government now plays a much bigger part in regulating people's lives. It also attempts to regulate people's attitudes. In the last part of the 20th century, laws were passed against discrimination, whether on grounds of race or gender. By making discrimination a crime, governments hoped to change people's attitudes.

## Racial discrimination

Over the centuries immigrants from many countries have come to Britain and black people have lived in Britain for many generations. However, during the 1950s new immigrants from the Caribbean, invited over to help Britain with a shortage of workers, faced discrimination. They found it difficult to get good housing, as landlords discriminated against them (Source 1); employers would not consider them for good jobs and they suffered many petty humiliations in pubs, hotels, etc. Right-wing political groups stirred up violence against them.

The government passed a number of laws making discrimination on grounds of race illegal (see Box below). They hoped that the law would also help to change attitudes by making it clear that Britain did not condone such discrimination. The Race Relations Board, later the Commission for Racial Equality, was set up to look at the situation and report on it. On the whole, the laws have removed the most blatant forms of discrimination, although it is obviously still practised.

### Race Relations Act, 1965

Made it illegal to practise discrimination in pubs, restaurants and hotels. Also illegal to stir up racial hatred. Set up the Race Relations Board.

### Race Relations Act, 1976

Set up the Commission for Racial Equality.

### SOURCE 1

Racial discrimination in housing. Private landlords in the 1950s putting up notices saying they would not let rooms to black people.

## Sex discrimination

Some women were given the vote in 1918 and all women got the right to vote on the same basis as men in 1928. This, however, did not bring about the total equality for women that many suffragettes expected. In politics, for example, out of over 600 MPs elected in 1945, only 24 were women.

At work, the situation was no better. Many jobs were closed to women entirely; few women were promoted to top jobs; women received lower pay for the same work or could only get low-paid work. In the Second World War, as in the First, women took on many vital jobs. But it was made clear that this was only temporary (Source 2). In the prosperous 1950s more and more women got jobs, but they were usually low-paid, boring ones (Source 3).

Women working on an assembly line in the 1950s.

**SOURCE 2**
Poster from just after the Second World War, encouraging women to stay at work for 'a little longer'.

WOMEN

*please lend your support a little longer....*

*let's work together for*

PROSPERITY

**SOURCE 4**

The lowest-paid sector of the workforce is made up of women. In 1976 43% of full-time women workers earned less than £40 a week, compared to only 5% of men. Despite the fact that women make up 40 to 50% of the workforce, the proportion of women in top jobs is low.

*From a Report by the Equal Opportunities Commission, 1978.*

Pressure from the women's movement pointed out all the injustice and inequality in this situation. It was only going to change by changing attitudes, especially men's attitudes. The government passed laws to prevent sex discrimination (see Box below).

The Equal Opportunities Commission was set up to report on the situation (Source 4).

On the whole, discrimination on grounds of sex seems to have been overcome more fully than racial discrimination. However, it is still present and women are still far from complete equality.

### Equal Pay Act, 1970

Men and women doing the same jobs should get the same pay.

### Sex Discrimination Act, 1975

All jobs were to be open to women on the same basis as men. The Equal Opportunities Commission was set up to observe the situation and report on it regularly.

❖ *From your own experience, is discrimination on grounds of race or gender still practised?*
❖ *What else do you think could be done to tackle it?*
❖ *Have the laws against discrimination changed attitudes, or have other factors been more important?*

## God as law-giver

Roots of early legal codes:
Hammurabi
Hebrews
Shari'ah, law of Islam

# RELIGION

## The Church as a special group of people

Church courts
Benefit of clergy

**God as judge**

Trial by ordeal

**Religion as an influence on society**

*Church courts*
Offences against religion, such as adultery, swearing, not going to Church

*Reform*
Prisons
Licensing laws

*Protest*
Pilgrimage of Grace
Heresy
Conscientious objectors

**Sanctuary**

119

# RAPID CHANGE: THE MODERN POLICE FORCE

## The police in about 1870

The 'Charley' (see page 64) in Source 1 may have been a bit of a curiosity by the time this picture was taken, but he reminds us that at that time the police were still only just taking over from a much older system.

**SOURCE 1**
The last of the 'Charleys', photographed in about 1870.

**SOURCE 2**
Tom Smith, a London policeman, 1856.

## 1870s

**1. Number of forces:** there were 239 separate police forces, each with their own rules, wages and conditions.

**2. The police constable.** Source 2 shows us what an early policeman looked like. The tall hat was strengthened so that he could stand on it to look over a high wall if necessary. The average wage was about 19/- (95p) a week. This put a policeman below the level of skilled workers, and most recruits were farm labourers or unskilled men. A policeman was not allowed to go out on his time off (and some forces worked a seven-day week). He could not take in a lodger to make ends meet, nor sell vegetables from his garden, own a dog, chickens or more than two pigs. He could not vote in elections. In some small police forces the policemen were also the firemen: there were two rows of hooks by the door and they grabbed the right uniform as they went out.

**3. Women.** There were no women police.

**4. Training.** His only training was some military drill.

**5. Communications.** He was on his own, with a whistle to call for help. Record-keeping was haphazard and local.

**6. Transport.** Apart from the River Thames Police, set up in 1798, police constables did their job on foot. The constable walked his beat, day and night, at a steady 2.5 mph, covering up to 20 miles, in all weathers.

**7. Special units.** Most forces had no special units, no detectives and no labs. In 1848 the Metropolitan Police appointed eight plain clothes detectives, but there was great suspicion of them.

## 1920s and 1930s

**1.** 188 police forces in 1890; 120 forces in 1946.

**2.** 1870 new uniform, with new-style helmet, something like the Prussian army helmet, but without the spike.

The 1890 Police Act set up a national system of pensions. Policemen now had a career structure and reasons for staying in the force. There was still dissatisfaction with wages, leading to two police strikes in 1918 and 1919. These brought an improvement in wages but also a ban on police going on strike.

**3.** First women police, 1920, at first to deal only with women and children, but see Source 4.

**4.** London police training college, 1907. National Police College started in 1947.

**5.** Telephones 1901; Radio 1910 (helped to catch Dr Crippen, see Source 3); Police telephone boxes (like Dr Who's Tardis), began in 1920s; 999 call started 1937.
National Criminal Record set up 1869.
Sir Edward Henry, from the Bengal Police, organised fingerprint records, 1901.

**6.** Bicycles 1909; cars 1919; motorbikes 1930s.

**7.** CID (Criminal Investigation Department) set up 1877.
1883 Special Irish Branch set up to deal with Irish terrorism (became Special Branch).
Flying Squad, to deal with serious theft, 1919.
Police Laboratory set up at Hendon, 1934–35.

NOTE: Some of the dates above are quite late; e.g. no forensic labs until 1935, no proper training of police until 1946. Furthermore, sometimes the dates can be misleading, e.g. police started to use cars in 1919, but few forces had many until well into the 1930s.

**SOURCE 4**
Women police motorcyclists deal with a drunk, 1940s.

**SOURCE 3**
Dr Crippen had murdered his wife and was fleeing to the USA on a liner with his mistress. The Captain was suspicious and radioed Scotland Yard, who sent a detective out by fast boat. Crippen was arrested on board. The picture shows him leaving the ship under arrest.

## Today

**1.** There are now only 41 police forces: a single force covering a large area is more efficient, reflecting how quickly criminals can move about the country.

**2.** Pay. Some still find the job a lonely one and leave because they find it difficult to make friends.

**3.** Women. The first woman Chief Constable, 1996.

**4.** All police are now trained for 14 weeks before starting. All forces now have specialist training facilities.

**5.** Police National Computer holds records of all vehicles, missing persons, fingerprints, etc.

**6.** See Sources 5 and 6. Most police constables do their jobs from patrol cars, and so are able to cover a wide area, but in many places police 'on the beat', walking the streets, have been restored.

**7.** As crime has become more complicated, so has crime prevention and detection, with many specialised units:
  Central Robbery Squad (formerly Flying Squad)
  Fraud Squad, 1946
  Special Patrol Group, 1965, became Metropolitan Patrol Group, 1987 (to deal with inner-city disturbances)
  Drugs Squad
  Dog Handlers, 1946
  Community Relations Branch, 1968
  Scene of Crime Officers: specialists in fingerprinting and forensic work
  Anti-terrorist Squad, 1971.

**SOURCE 5**
Police helicopter of the Air Support Unit, fitted with TV cameras, searchlights and public address system.

**SOURCE 6**
Motorway patrol car.

# SLOW CHANGE: THE COURTROOM

**Royal coat-of-arms.** Symbol of the authority given to the court, derived from the monarch.

Judge's full-bottomed wig, as worn by older men in the early 18th century

Barrister's short wig, as worn by younger men in the early 18th century.

**Jury.** The roots of the jury system are at least 1,000 years old. Men on oath appeared in Anglo-Saxon courts (see page 19). Norman kings also used sworn juries to get at the truth in legal matters. The jury as the body which decides whether the accused is guilty or not guilty began under Henry II in 1164.

**The dock.** A 16th-century word for the place where the accused stands in court.

**Language.** Several old-fashioned phrases are still used: the judge is called 'My Lord' (said as 'M'Lud'), women are always addressed as 'Ma'am', etc.

## Procedure

The basic English trial procedure has changed very little since medieval times:

The charge is read to the accused, who is asked whether he or she pleads guilty or not guilty. The prosecution gives their 'case', their version of what happened. Then the defence gives their version. Either side may call witnesses to support their case. The judge sums up. The jury makes their decision. If the accused is guilty, the judge decides the punishment.

## Changes

Of course there have been changes:

Up to the late 19th century the person who had suffered from the crime – been robbed, or cheated, or assaulted – had to bring the prosecution personally. This meant that most cases consisted simply of accuser and accused facing each other in court. The accused had often been in prison before the trial and so may not have known exactly what the charge was, who was to be called as a witness, and so on. Most cases only lasted a few minutes.

● **Prosecutions.** By the late 19th century the police were taking over more and more of the job of bringing prosecutions. In the 20th century the Crown Prosecution Service has done this.

● **Barristers** began to be used in the 18th century, mainly by the prosecution, but for many years they were a rarity, only appearing in the most complex cases. By the late 19th century barristers were more common, usually appearing for the prosecution, as defendants were too poor to afford the fees. From 1903 poor defendants could have their fees paid for in serious cases. Legal Aid was set up in 1974 and now it is rare for someone to conduct their own case.

● **JPs.** In 1918 women began to be appointed as JPs. JPs now have to be trained and as part of their training have to visit each of the places to which they could send offenders: prison, detention centre, etc. Judges do not have to do this.

● The **Court of Appeal** was set up in 1907.

● **Crown Courts** were set up in 1971, replacing Assize and Quarter sessions with regular courts in major towns and cities. In some Crown Courts, JPs sit alongside a judge.

Published by Collins Educational
An imprint of HarperCollins*Publishers* Ltd
77–85 Fulham Palace Road
London W6 8JB

© HarperCollinsPublishers Ltd 1997
First published 1997

ISBN 0 00 327321-0

Christopher Culpin asserts the moral right to be identified as the author of this work.

All rights reserved. No part of this publication may be reproduced, stored in a retrieval system, or transmitted in any form or by any means, electronic, mechanical, photocopying, recording or otherwise, without either the prior permission of the Publisher or a licence permitting restricted copying in the United Kingdom issued by the Copyright Licensing Agency Ltd, 90 Tottenham Court Road, London W1P 9HE.

British Library Cataloguing in Publication Data
A catalogue record for this book is available from the British Library.

Edited by Lorimer Poultney
Design by Sally Boothroyd
Cover design by Derek Lee
Illustrations by Peter Bull Art Studio (pp. 4, 5, 6); Robert Ashby (p. 124–125), Lorimer Poultney (pp. 43, 60, 77, 88)
Picture research by Caroline Thompson
Production by Susan Cashin
Printed and bound by Scotprint Ltd, Musselburgh.

ACKNOWLEDGEMENTS
Every effort has been made to contact the holders of copyright material, but if any have been inadvertently overlooked the publishers will be pleased to make the necessary arrangements at the first opportunity.

The publishers would like to thank the following for permission to reproduce photographs (T = Top, B = Bottom, C = Centre, L= Left, R = Right).

The Ancient Art and Architecture Collection Ltd 12; Bodleian Library, University of Oxford (MS Bodl. 264, f. 81V) 25, (4° E. 17 Art. 13) 37T;

The British Library (Cott, Nero D.IV f. 29) 18, (Royal MS 2B VII f. 78V) 24, (Addn MS 62925 f. 86) 26, (MS Harl. 4380 f. 6) 27, (Royal 6 E VI f. 128V. miniature) 31; The British Museum 67; The Dean and Chapter of Canterbury 22; J. Allan Cash Ltd 87, 90T, 123B; Conway Library, Courtauld Institute/The Master and Fellows of Corpus Christi College, Cambridge 30; Mary Evans Picture Library 15, 29L, 52, 61, 77, 81, 100T; Fitzwilliam Museum, Cambridge 35; The Fotomas Index 29R, 36, 38, 42, 43, 44, 45, 47, 49T, 50, 53, 56, 64, 83, 111, 112B; John Frost Historical Newspaper Service 62, 100B; The Hulton Getty Picture Collection 14, 20, 37B, 54, 55, 65, 68, 69, 71, 73, 84, 88, 94, 102, 103, 106, 107, 116, 117T, 120, 121; Gloucester Jail 70; Ronald Grant Archive 28, 57; Guildhall Library, Corporation of London 66; Sonia Halliday Photographs 32; Hirmer Fotoarchiv 13; Michael Holford 10, 17; Steve Jones 72; Chief Constable, Lincolnshire Police 60; Manchester Public Libraries 59; Mansell Collection 21; Metropolitan Police Service 123T; Museum of London 76; Museum of Welsh Life 112T; National Portrait Gallery, London 49B; J. Olley/Network Photographers 3L; J. Green/Network Photographers 95T; M. Abrahams/Network Photographers 98; D. Doran/Network Photographers 98T, 109; Peace Pledge Union 105; Popperfoto/Reuter 89; Popperfoto 90B; Popperfoto/Reuter 99B; Lorimer Poultney 9; PA News 3R, 91, 92TR, 93; Public Record Office 78; Rex Features 95B; Gavin Rowe 39; RCHME © Crown Copyright 23, 41; Rural History Centre, University of Reading 114; Caroline Thompson 96.

**Cover Photograph:** Shout Photos